The Inspiration and Truth
of Sacred Scripture

The Inspiration and Truth of Sacred Scripture

The Word That Comes from God and Speaks of God for the Salvation of the World

Pontifical Biblical Commission

Translated by
Thomas Esposito, OCist, and Stephen Gregg, OCist

Reviewed by
Fearghus O'Fearghail

Foreword by
Cardinal Gerhard Ludwig Müller

LITURGICAL PRESS
Collegeville, Minnesota

www.litpress.org

This work was translated from the Italian, *Inspirazione e Verità della Sacra Scrittura. La parola che viene da Dio e parla di Dio per salvare il mondo* (Libreria Editrice Vaticana, 2014).

Cover design by Jodi Hendrickson. Cover photo: Dreamstime.

Excerpts from documents of the Second Vatican Council are from *The Documents of Vatican II*, edited by Walter M. Abbott, SJ (New York: The America Press, 1966).

Unless otherwise noted, Scripture texts in this work are taken from the *New Revised Standard Version Bible* © 1989, Division of Christian Education of the National Council of the Churches of Christ in the United States of America. Used by permission. All rights reserved.

Library of Congress Control Number: 2014937336

ISBN: 978-0-8146-4903-9   978-0-8146-4904-6 (ebook)

Table of Contents

Part Three

The Interpretation of the Word of God and Its Challenges   123

Foreword

The life of the Church is founded on the Word of God. This Word is passed down in Sacred Scripture, namely, in the writings of the Old and New Testaments. According to the faith of the Church, all of these writings are inspired; they have God, who made use of human beings chosen by him for their composition, as their ultimate author. On account of their divine inspiration, the biblical books communicate the truth. Their whole value for the life and mission of the Church depends on their inspiration and truth. Writings which do not originate in God cannot communicate the Word of God, and writings which are not true cannot establish and animate the life and mission of the Church. Nevertheless, the truth present in the sacred texts is not always easily recognizable. At times, there are at least apparent contrasts between what is read in the biblical accounts and the findings of the natural and historical sciences. These sciences appear to contradict what the biblical writings affirm and place their truth in doubt. It is obvious that this situation also concerns biblical inspiration: if what is communicated in the Bible is not true, how can it have God for its author? Beginning from such questions, the Pontifical Biblical Commission set out to investigate the relationship between inspiration and truth and to verify how the biblical writings themselves address these concepts. First of all, it must be acknowledged that the sacred writings rarely speak about inspiration directly (cf. 2 Tim 3:16; 2 Pet 1:20-21); they do, however, continually attest a relationship between their human authors and God and in that way express their provenance from God. In the Old Testament, the relationship linking the human author to God and vice versa is attested in diverse forms and has varying characteristics. In the New Testament, every relationship with God is mediated by the person of Jesus, the Messiah and Son of God. He, the Word of God made visible (cf. John 1:1, 14), is the mediator of all that comes from God.

In the Bible, we encounter many and various themes. An attentive reading, however, shows that the primary and dominating theme is God and his salvific plan for human beings. The truth which we find in Sacred Scripture essentially concerns God and his relationship with his creatures. In the New Testament, the fundamental definition of this bond is found in the words of Jesus: "I am the way, and the truth, and the life. No one comes to the Father except through me" (John 14:6). As the incarnate Word of God (cf. John 1:14), Jesus Christ is the perfect truth about God; he reveals God as Father and offers access to him, the source of all life. The other definitions of God in the biblical writings are oriented toward the Word of God made man in Jesus Christ. This incarnate word becomes the key to their interpretation.

After treating the concept of inspiration witnessed to in the biblical books, in the relationship between God and the human authors, and in the truth which these writings entrust to us, the Biblical Commission goes on to examine a number of texts that pose difficulties for interpreters from historical and ethical-social points of view. To respond to the questions that arise in the interpretation of these difficult texts, it is necessary to study them carefully, taking into account the findings of the modern sciences and, simultaneously, the main theme of the texts, namely, God and his plan of salvation. Such an approach shows how the doubts raised against their truth and origin in God can be resolved.

The present document of the Biblical Commission does not constitute an official declaration of the Church's Magisterium on this topic, nor does it intend to set forth a complete doctrine regarding inspiration and the truth of Sacred Scripture. It only wishes to report the results of an attentive exegetical study of the biblical texts regarding their origin in God and their truth. The conclusions here are offered to the other theological disciplines, to be completed and deepened according to their own particular perspectives.

I thank the members of the Biblical Commission for their patience and competence, and I express my desire that their work may contribute to a more attentive, appreciative, and joyful listening to Sacred Scripture in the Church as the Word coming from God and speaking of God for the life of the world.

His Eminence, Cardinal Gerhard Ludwig Müller
President, Pontifical Biblical Commission
February 22, 2014
Feast of the Chair of Saint Peter

General Introduction

For as the rain and the snow come down from heaven, and do not return there until they have watered the earth, making it bring forth and sprout, giving seed to the sower and bread to the eater, so shall my word be that goes out from my mouth; it shall not return to me empty, but it shall accomplish that which I purpose, and succeed in the thing for which I sent it.

–Isaiah 55:10-11[1]

Long ago God spoke to our ancestors in many and various ways by the prophets, but in these last days he has spoken to us by a Son, whom he appointed heir of all things, through whom he also created the worlds.

–Hebrews 1:1-2

1. The theme "The Word of God in the Life and Mission of the Church" was assigned to the 2008 Synod of Bishops. In his Post-Synodal Apostolic Exhortation *Verbum Domini*, the Holy Father Benedict XVI returned to the topics of the Synod and considered them at greater depth. In particular, he emphasizes: "Certainly theological reflection has always considered inspiration and truth as two

---

[1] Unless directly translated from the original document, all Scripture quotes are taken from the *New Revised Standard Version* (NRSV); all quotes from the documents of Vatican II are from Walter Abbott, *The Documents of Vatican II*; and those from *Verbum Domini* are from the Vatican website.

key concepts for an ecclesial hermeneutic of the sacred Scriptures. Nonetheless, one must acknowledge the need today for a fuller and more adequate study of these realities, in order to respond better to the necessity of interpreting the sacred texts in accordance with their nature. Here I would express my fervent hope that research in this field will progress and bear fruit, both for biblical science and for the spiritual life of the faithful" (n. 19). In response to the Holy Father's desire, the Pontifical Biblical Commission seeks to make a contribution toward a more adequate understanding of the concepts of inspiration and truth, fully aware that this corresponds in a special way to the nature of the Bible and to its significance for the life of the Church.

The liturgical assembly is the most significant and solemn place for the proclamation of the Word of God, and it is where all the faithful encounter the Bible. In the eucharistic worship, which consists of two principal parts—the Liturgy of the Word and the Liturgy of the Eucharist (see *Sacrosanctum Concilium*, n. 56)—the Church celebrates "the paschal mystery: reading 'in all the scriptures the things referring to himself' (Luke 24:27), celebrating the Eucharist in which 'the victory and triumph of his death are again made present,' and at the same time giving thanks 'to God for his unspeakable gift' (2 Cor 9:15) in Christ Jesus, 'to the praise of his glory' (Eph 1:12), through the power of the Holy Spirit" (*Sacrosanctum Concilium*, n. 6).

The presence of Jesus, revealer of God the Father in his word and salvific work, and the union of the community of the faithful with him are at the center of this assembly. The purpose of the whole celebration is to make Jesus present in the midst of the community of believers and to facilitate the encounter and union with him and with God the Father. Christ in his paschal mystery is proclaimed in the reading of the Word of God and celebrated in the eucharistic liturgy.

I. The Liturgy of the Word and Its Eucharistic Setting

2. Every week on Sunday, that is, on the Lord's Day, which the Church considers "the original feast day" (*Sacrosanctum Concilium*,

n. 106), the resurrection of Christ is celebrated with special joy and solemnity. On this day, on which "richer fare [must] be provided for the faithful at the table of God's Word" (*Sacrosanctum Concilium*, n. 51), several psalm verses are sung and three biblical passages are proclaimed, with one usually taken from the Old Testament, one from the non-gospel writings of the New Testament, and one from the four gospels. After the reading of each of the first two passages, the reader says, "The Word of the Lord," and the faithful respond, "Thanks be to God." At the end of the proclamation of the gospel, the deacon or priest declares, "The Gospel of the Lord," and the people respond, "Praise to you, Lord Jesus Christ." Two characteristics of reading and listening are highlighted by this brief dialogue. The reader emphasizes the importance of this action and reminds the listeners to be fully aware that what has been communicated to them is truly the Word of God or, more specifically, the Word of the Lord (Jesus), who in his very person is the Word of God (see John 1:1-2). The faithful, for their part, manifest the attitude of humble reverence with which they receive the word that God directs to them: full of gratitude, they listen with praise and joy to the Good News of the Lord Jesus.

Even if these characteristics are not always realized perfectly, the Liturgy of the Word constitutes a privileged moment of communication: God in his kindness addresses himself to his people with human words, and they receive the Word of God with thanksgiving and praise. In the Liturgy of the Word, and most of all in the Liturgy of the Eucharist, the paschal mystery of Christ, the summit and fulfillment of God's communication with humanity, is celebrated. In this communication, the redemption of human beings is achieved and, at the same time, the highest and most perfect glorification of God. The celebration is not a ritual formality, since its objective is to enable the faithful to "learn to offer themselves too. Through Christ the Mediator, they should be drawn day by day into ever closer union with God and with each other, so that finally God may be all in all" (*Sacrosanctum Concilium*, n. 48). The fact that God addresses his word to human beings in the history of salvation and that he sends his Son, who is his Word incarnate (John 1:14), has this single purpose: to offer human beings union with himself.

II. The Context for the Study of the Inspiration and Truth of the Bible

3. On the basis of what we have stated so far about the Word of God in the Liturgy of the Word and in connection with the eucharistic celebration, we can say that we listen to it in a theological, Christological, soteriological, and ecclesiological context. God offers salvation in a definitive and complete way in his Christ, bringing about communion between himself and his human creatures, who are represented by his Church. This setting, which is the most appropriate setting for the proclamation of Sacred Scripture, also constitutes the most adequate context for studying its inspiration and truth. After the proclamation of the biblical passages, as we have said, the affirmation that they are "the Word of God" (or "Word of the Lord") always follows. This affirmation can be understood in a double sense: first of all, as a word that comes from God, but also as a word that speaks of God. These two meanings are closely connected with each other. Only God knows God; consequently, only God can speak of God in an adequate and reliable way. Therefore, only a word that comes from God can rightly speak about God. The affirmation "the Word of the Lord" invites the faithful to be mindful of what they are hearing and to pay it appropriate attention. They must have the reverence and gratitude due to the word that comes from God, and they should be attentive to grasp and to understand what this word communicates about God and thus enter into an ever more living union with him.

Our document, which has as its title *The Inspiration and Truth of Sacred Scripture*, will develop these two aspects. When we declare that the Bible is inspired, we affirm that all its books "have God as their author and have been handed on as such to the Church herself" (*Dei Verbum*, n. 11). In our study of the inspiration of the Bible, we set ourselves the task of establishing what the biblical writings themselves say about their divine provenance. As regards the truth of the Bible, we must above all be aware that although it covers many different subjects, the Bible really has a primary and central theme: God himself and salvation. There are many other documentary sources and many other disciplines providing reliable information on questions of every kind; the Bible, insofar as it is the

Word of God, is the authoritative source for knowledge about God. For the Dogmatic Constitution *Dei Verbum* of the Second Vatican Council, God himself and his project of salvation for humankind are the content of his revelation by antonomasia. Indeed, in the very first chapter of this conciliar text, it is stated: "In his goodness and wisdom, God chose to reveal himself and to make known to us the hidden purpose of his will (cf. Eph 1:9) by which through Christ, the Word made flesh, man might in the Holy Spirit have access to the Father and come to share in the divine nature (cf. Eph 2:18; 2 Pet 1:4)" (*Dei Verbum*, n. 2). The Bible is at the service of the transmission of revelation (cf. *Dei Verbum*, nn. 7–10). Therefore, as we study the truth of the Bible, we will focus our attention on precisely this question: what do the various biblical writings say about God and his project of salvation?

III. The Three Parts of the Document

4. The first part of our document deals with the inspiration of Sacred Scripture, investigating its provenance from God, while the second part studies the truth of the Word of God, highlighting the message about God and his project of salvation. We hope, on the one hand, to increase awareness that this word comes from God and, on the other, to focus the attention of hearers and readers of the Bible on that which God, for his part, wishes to communicate to us about himself and about his salvific plan for human beings. With the same attitude with which we celebrate the paschal mystery of Christ as the mystery of God and of our salvation, we are invited to receive the word that God, full of love and kindness, addresses to us. The goal is to receive, in communion with other believers, the gift of being able to hear and to understand what he discloses about himself, in order to renew and deepen our personal relationship with him.

The third part of the document goes on to deal with some challenges that arise from the Bible itself, because of certain aspects that appear to contradict its quality of being the Word of God. Here we point out in particular two challenges which confront the reader. The first derives from the enormous progress in the last two centuries of knowledge about the history, culture, and languages of the peoples of the ancient Near East, which constituted the environment of Israel and of its Sacred Scriptures. It is not rare that there are strong contrasts between the data from these disciplines and what we can garner from the biblical account, if it is read according to the model of a chronicle giving an exact account of events, let alone in strict chronological order. These contrasts pose an initial difficulty and raise the question of whether the reader can trust the historical truth of the biblical accounts.

Another challenge arises from the fact that many biblical texts are full of violence. We can cite, by way of example, the cursing psalms and also the order given by God to Israel to exterminate entire populations. Christian readers are upset and confused by such texts. Furthermore, there are non-Christian readers who rebuke Christians for having terrifying passages in their sacred texts and accuse them of professing and propagating a religion that inspires violence.

The third part of the document intends to confront these and other interpretive challenges, showing, on the one hand, how to overcome fundamentalism (cf. Pontifical Biblical Commission, *The Interpretation of the Bible in the Church*; cf. *EB* 1381–90) and, on the other, how to avoid skepticism. By removing these obstacles, the way will hopefully be cleared for a mature and proper reception of the Word of God.

This text, then, intends to make a contribution so that, through a deeper understanding of the concepts of inspiration and truth, the Word of God can be received by all, in the liturgical assembly and in every other place, in a way that corresponds ever more closely to this unique gift of God, in which he communicates his very self and invites man and woman into communion with him.

Part One

The Testimony of the Biblical Writings on Their Origin from God

I. Introduction

5. In the first section, we examine what the Dogmatic Constitution *Dei Verbum* of the Second Vatican Council and the Post-Synodal Apostolic Exhortation *Verbum Domini* understand by revelation and inspiration, the two divine actions that are fundamental in characterizing Sacred Scripture as the Word of God. We will then show how the biblical writings manifest their provenance from God; for the New Testament we have the added distinctiveness that there is no relationship with God except through Jesus. We will conclude with a reflection on the criteria that are relevant for investigating the testimony of the biblical writings with regard to their provenance from God.

1.1 Revelation and Inspiration in Dei Verbum *and* Verbum Domini

On *revelation, Dei Verbum* [*DV*] says, "In his goodness and wisdom, God chose to reveal himself and to make known to us the hidden purpose of his will (cf. Eph 1:9) by which through Christ, the Word made flesh, man might in the Holy Spirit have access to the Father and come to share in the divine nature (see Eph 2:18; 2 Pet 1:4)" (n. 2). God reveals himself in a "plan of revelation" (*DV*, n. 2). He manifests himself in creation: "God, who through the Word creates all things (cf. John 1:3) and keeps them in existence, gives men an enduring witness to himself in created realities (cf. Rom 1:19-20)" (*DV*, n. 3; cf. *Verbum Domini* [*VD*], n. 8). God reveals himself especially in man, created "in his image" (Gen 1:27; cf. *VD*, n. 9). Revelation is realized, then, "by deeds and words having an inner unity" (*DV*, n. 2), in the salvation history of the people of Israel (*DV*, nn. 3, 14–16), and reaches its peak "in Christ, who is both the mediator and the fullness of all revelation" (*DV*, n. 2; cf. *DV*, nn. 4, 17–20). Speaking of its Trinitarian dimension, *Verbum Domini* 20 says: "The revelation of God the Father culminates in the Son's gift of the Paraclete (cf. John 14:16), the Spirit of the Father and the Son, who guides us 'into all the truth' (John 16:13)."

Inspiration strictly concerns the books of Sacred Scripture. *Dei Verbum*, which calls God "the inspirer and author of both Testaments" (n. 16), asserts in a more detailed way that "in composing the sacred books, God chose men, and while employed by him, they made use of their powers and abilities, so that with him acting in them and through them, they, as true authors, consigned to writing everything and only those things which he wanted" (n. 11). Inspiration as an activity of God, therefore, directly concerns the human authors: they are the ones who are personally inspired. But then the writings composed by them are also called inspired (*DV*, nn. 11, 14).

1.2 The Biblical Writings and Their Divine Provenance

6. We have seen that God is the only author of revelation and that the books of Sacred Scripture, which serve for the transmission of divine revelation, are inspired by him. God is the "author" of these books (*DV*, n. 16), but through human beings whom he has chosen. These do not write under dictation but are "true authors" (*DV*, n. 11) who employ their own faculties and abilities. *Dei Verbum* 11 does not specify in detail what this relationship is between the authors and God, even if it refers in its notes (nn. 18–20) to a traditional explanation based on principal and instrumental causality.

Turning to the biblical books and exploring what they themselves say about their inspiration, we recognize that, in the Bible, only two New Testament writings speak explicitly of divine inspiration, and they relate it to some writings of the Old Testament. In 2 Timothy 3:16 it is said: "All scripture is inspired by God and is useful for teaching, for reproof, for correction, and for training in righteousness." And 2 Peter 1:20-21 affirms: "First of all you must understand this, that no prophecy of scripture is a matter of one's own interpretation, because no prophecy ever came by human will, but men and women moved by the Holy Spirit spoke from God." The rare occurrence of the term "inspiration" means that we cannot limit our research to such a restricted semantic field.

Studying the biblical texts closely, however, we perceive a noteworthy fact: the relationship between their authors and God is constantly made explicit. This happens in various ways, each of them capable of making it clear that the respective writings come from God. The task of our investigation will be to identify in the texts of Sacred Scripture the indications of the relationship between human authors and God, showing thereby the divine provenance of these books, in other words, their inspiration. We intend to present a kind of phenomenology of the "God–human author" relationship, as regards the manner in which this relationship is attested in the pages of the Bible, thus highlighting their character as a word that comes from God. In this document, then, the PBC does not intend to demonstrate the fact of the inspiration of the biblical writings, which is a task for fundamental theology. We begin, rather, from the truth of faith according to which the books of Sacred Scripture are inspired by God and communicate his Word; our contribution will be only to clarify their nature, as it appears from the testimony of the writings themselves.

We can call "witness to themselves" that particular phenomenon of the biblical books which attests the relationship of their authors with God and their provenance from God. This specific testimony will be the focus of our investigations.

7. The Church documents we have cited several times (*Dei Verbum* and *Verbum Domini*) distinguish between "revelation" and "inspiration" as two distinct divine actions. "Revelation" is presented as the fundamental act of God by which he communicates who he is and the mystery of his will (cf. *DV*, n. 2), at the same time

rendering human beings capable of receiving revelation. "Inspiration," however, is presented as the action by which God enables certain persons, chosen by him, to transmit his revelation faithfully in writing (cf. *DV*, n. 11). Inspiration presupposes revelation and is at the service of the faithful transmission of revelation in the biblical writings.

From the testimony of the biblical writings, we can gather only a few indications about the specific relationship between the human author and God with regard to the activity of writing. Therefore, the phenomenology that we are about to present concerning both the relationship between the human author and God, as well as the divine provenance of the written texts, presents a rather general and varied picture. We will see that the specific concept of inspiration is hardly ever specified in the Scriptures and does not even receive an explanation there. This is due to the particular nature of the testimony of the various biblical books; indeed, if, on the one hand, the texts constantly make clear the divine provenance of their content and message, on the other hand, they say little or nothing about the way in which they were written or about themselves as written documents. Consequently, the broad concept of revelation and the more specific one of its written attestation (inspiration) are seen as a single process. Very often they are spoken of in such a way that one is meant along with the other. Nevertheless, the simple fact that the declarations we have cited come from the written texts makes it clear that their authors implicitly affirm that their texts constitute the final expression and stable deposit of the revelatory acts of God.

1.3 The Writings of the New Testament and Their Relationship to Jesus

8. As regards the writings of the New Testament, we observe a particular situation: they manifest a relationship of their authors with God only through the person of Jesus. Jesus himself expresses the cause of this phenomenon very precisely: "No one comes to the Father except through me" (John 14:6), an affirmation based on the unique knowledge that the Son has of the Father (cf. Matt 11:27; Luke 10:22; John 1:18).

The behavior of Jesus with his disciples is significant and instructive. The gospels illustrate the formation that he gives them in which the relationship with Jesus and with God that is essential for an apostle's words or an evangelist's writing to become "the Word of God" appears in a paradigmatic way. According to our sources, Jesus did not write anything himself, and he did not dictate anything to his disciples. What he did can be summarized in this way: he called some men to follow him, to share his life, to assist in his activity, to acquire an ever deeper knowledge of his person, to grow in faith in him and in communion of life with him. This is the gift that Jesus gave his disciples, his way of preparing them to be his apostles, who proclaim his message. Their word is such that Jesus characterizes future Christians as "those who will believe in me through their word" (John 17:20). And he says to his missionaries: "Whoever listens to you listens to me, and whoever rejects you rejects me, and whoever rejects me rejects the one who sent me" (Luke 10:16; cf. John 15:20). The word of his messengers can be the foundation of the faith of all Christians because, coming from the most intimate union with Jesus, it is the word of Jesus. The personal relationship with the Lord Jesus, practiced with a living and informed faith in his person, constitutes the basic foundation for this "inspiration" that makes the apostles capable of communicating, in speech or in writing, the message of Jesus, "the Word of God." The proclamation of his gospel, not the communication of words literally pronounced by Jesus, is decisive. A typical example of this is the Gospel of John, every word of which is said to manifest the style of John and at the same time to communicate faithfully what Jesus said.

9. Here we outline, precisely on the basis of the Gospel of John, an intimate connection between the nature of the relationship with Jesus and with God (inspiration) and the content of the message that is communicated as the Word of God (truth). The central message of Jesus according to the Gospel of John is this: God the Father and his boundless love for the world, revealed in his Son (cf. John 3:16); this corresponds to *Dei Verbum*, n. 2, God and his salvation. This message cannot be received or understood with a cognitive approach that is solely intellectual or merely one of rote learning, but only in an intensely living and personal relationship, that is, according to

that same relationship with which Jesus formed his disciples. One can always speak in a formal and correct way about God and his love, but only in living faith in him and in his love can one receive the gift of God and give witness to it. It is evident, therefore, that the central message (truth) and the manner of receiving it, in order to attest it (inspiration), mutually condition each other; in either case, we are dealing with the most intense and personal communion of life with the Father, revealed in Jesus—a communion of life which is salvation.

1.4 Criteria for Demonstrating the Relationship with God in the Biblical Writings

10. According to what we have gathered from the gospels, living faith in Jesus, the Son of God, is the principal goal of the formation given by Jesus to his disciples, and in this faith their fundamental relationship with Jesus and with God is expressed. This faith is a gift of the Holy Spirit (cf. John 3:5; 16:13) and is lived in an intimate, conscious, and personal union with the Father and the Son (cf. John 17:20-23). By means of this faith, the disciples are united to the person of Jesus, who is "the mediator and the fullness of all revelation" (*DV*, n. 2), and they receive from him the elements of their apostolic testimony in its oral or written expression. Because it comes from Jesus, the Word of God, such testimony can only be a word that comes from God. The personal relationship of faith (1) with the source through which God reveals himself (2) are the two decisive elements which guarantee that the words and deeds of the apostles come from God.

Jesus is "the culmination of the revelation of God the Father" (*Verbum Domini*, n. 20), a culmination preceded by a rich "economy" of divine revelation. As we have already noted, God reveals himself in creation (*DV*, n. 3) and especially in humanity, created "in his image" (Gen 1:27). He reveals himself above all in the history of the people of Israel "by deeds and words having an inner unity" (*DV*, n. 2). Outlined in this way are various forms of God's revelation, which reaches its fullness and culmination in the person of Jesus (Heb 1:1-2).

In the case of the gospels (and more generally for the apostolic writings), the two elements decisive for provenance from God are (1) living faith in Jesus and (2) the person of Jesus who is the culmination of divine revelation. In our study of the divine provenance of the other biblical writings, two criteria will serve as a test: what personal faith in God (according to the specific phase of the "plan" of revelation) and what forms of his revelation manifest themselves in the various writings? The respective biblical writing comes from God through its author's living faith in God and through the relationship of this author with a specific form (or with different forms) of divine revelation. It is not rare that a biblical text bases itself on an earlier inspired text and participates in this way in the same divine provenance.

With these criteria, one can usefully explore the testimony of the various biblical writings and see how, for example, legal texts, wisdom sayings, prophetic oracles, prayers of all kinds, apostolic admonitions, etc., come from God; God, therefore, by means of the human authors, is their author. It is clear that the concrete mode of divine provenance is different, as the case may be, and cannot be compared to a simple and uniform divine dictate. Nevertheless, what is constantly attested is the human author's personal faith in God and his obedience to the various forms of divine revelation.

In this way, as we study the biblical writings themselves and explore their witness to the relationship of their authors with God, we shall seek to demonstrate more concretely how inspiration presents itself as a relationship between God, inspirer and author, and human beings, true authors chosen by God.

II. The Testimony of Select Old Testament Texts

11. We have chosen a number of books representative of the Old and New Testaments to illustrate how their origin from God is expressed in the texts themselves. For the Old Testament, we will follow the classical division of Law, Prophets, and Writings (cf. Luke 24:44); we have chosen, therefore, for our investigation the Pentateuch, the prophets and the historical books (also called the "early prophets"), and, finally, the Psalms and the book of Sirach.

2.1 The Pentateuch

The idea of a divine origin of the biblical texts is developed in the accounts of the Pentateuch on the basis of the concept of writing, or setting something down in writing. Thus, at particularly significant moments, Moses receives from God the task of putting into writing, for example, the founding document of the Covenant (Exod 24:4), or the text of its renewal (Exod 34:27); elsewhere he seems to fulfill the sense of these instructions, putting other relevant things into writing (Exod 17:14; Num 33:2; Deut 31:22), to the composition of the entire Torah (cf. Deut 27:3, 8; 31:9). The book of Deuteronomy gives particular importance to the specific role of Moses, presenting him as an inspired mediator of revelation and authorized interpreter of the divine Word. From this starting point, the traditional idea naturally developed that Moses was the author of the Pentateuch, so that the books of Moses not only speak of him but are even held to be his compositions.

The principal affirmations about God's self-communication are found in the stories of Israel's encounter with him on the mountain of God, Sinai/Horeb (Exod 19–Num 10; Deut 5ff.). These stories seek to express, with suggestive images, the idea that God is the origin of the biblical testimony. One can say, therefore, that the basis for understanding the Bible as the Word of God was set at Sinai, because there God constituted Moses as the single mediator of his revelation. It falls to Moses to put into writing the divine revelation so that he can transmit it and preserve it as the Word of God for people of all times. The written form not only makes the transmission of the Word possible but also clearly raises the question about the human author. This, in the case of the Bible, leads to its self-awareness as the Word of God in human words. This idea (see *DV*, n. 12) is already expressed in essence in Exodus 19:19, where it is said that God answered Moses "with a voice"; thus it is clear that God "condescends" to use human language, also (and especially) when dealing with the mediator of his revelation.

12. Moreover, the divine origin of the written word is subtly enhanced in the Sinai account. In this context, the Decalogue appears as a unique and incomparable document. It can be considered as the point of departure for the idea of the divine origin of Sacred

Scripture (inspiration), because *as a text* only the Decalogue is connected with the idea of having been *written by God himself* (cf. Exod 24:12; 31:18; 32:16; 34:1, 28; Deut 4:13; 9:10; 10:4). This text, which God himself wrote on two tablets of stone, is the basis for the concept of a divine origin of the biblical texts. This concept is developed in two directions by the narrative of the Pentateuch. On the one hand, the special authority that belongs to the Decalogue comes to light as compared with all the other laws and instructions of the Bible; on the other, it is evident that the concept of "scripture" (in the sense of something set down in writing) is connected in a special way to the mediator of revelation, Moses; later on, in fact, "Moses" and the Pentateuch are interchangeable terms.

As to the first aspect, that of the Decalogue written by God himself, it should be noted that the transmission and reception of this particular text are affirmed in the tradition of Sacred Scripture independently of its material frame consisting of the two tablets of stone. It is not the tablets on which God wrote that were preserved and venerated but the text that God wrote that becomes part of Sacred Scripture (cf. Exod 20; Deut 5).

The Ten Commandments that God put in writing and consigned to Moses—and here we come to the second aspect—point to the special relationship between God and humanity as far as Sacred Scripture is concerned. Moses, in fact, is not instituted as mediator by virtue of a divine plan, but God accedes to the prayers of human beings (Israel) who request a mediator. After God had addressed the people of Israel directly (Exod 19), the people ask Moses to act as mediator, since they fear the direct encounter with God (Exod 20:18-21). God then accedes to the will of the people and institutes Moses as mediator, speaking with him and communicating his instructions to him in detail (Exod 20:22–23:33). In the end, Moses commits these words to writing, for through them God stipulates his covenant with Israel (Exod 24:3-8). To confirm this event, God promises to give Moses the tablets on which God himself had written (Exod 24:12). It could not be expressed in a clearer and more profound way that Sacred Scripture, handed on through generations by the community of faith of Jews and of Christians, has its origin in God, even though and because it happened that it was written by humans. This self-attestation of Sacred Scripture reaches its completion when, at the end of the Pentateuch, it is affirmed that Moses himself set down in writing the instruction imparted to the people of Israel before entering the promised land (see Deut 31:9), giving it to the people as a program for the life they would lead there in the future. Only when human beings let themselves be engaged by this word of Sacred Scripture, which is addressed to them, can they recognize it and receive it "not as a human word, but as it really is, God's word, which is also at work in you believers" (1 Thess 2:13).

2.2 The Prophetic and Historical Books

13. The prophetic and historical books are, along with the Pentateuch, the parts of the Old Testament that insist most on the divine origin of their content. In general, God addresses himself to his people or to its leaders through human beings: Moses, the archetype of the prophets in the Pentateuch (Deut 18:18-22), the prophets in the prophetic and historical books. We will seek to show how the prophetic and historical books affirm the divine origin of their content.

2.2.1 The Prophetic Books: Collections of What the Lord Said to His People through His Messengers

The prophetic books present themselves as collections of what the Lord said to his people through the (presumed) "authors" who give their names to the collections. Indeed, these books declare insistently that the Lord is the author of their content. And they do so with various introductory or interposed expressions in the discourse. These expressions assert, or presume, that the prophetic books are discourses of the Lord, and they specify that the Lord addresses himself to his people through the authors of the books in question. In fact, much of the prophetic books is placed formally on the Lord's lips. At the same time, these books present their authors as persons whom the Lord has sent with the task of transmitting a message to his people.

a) The "Prophetic Formulae"

The titles of two-thirds of the prophetic books explicitly affirm that they are of divine origin by means of "the formula of the 'coming' of the word of the Lord." Prescinding from differences in detail, the formula can be summarized in the affirmation "The word of the Lord came to . . ." followed by the name of the prophet who receives the word (as in the books of Jeremiah, Ezekiel, Hosea, Joel, Jonah, Zephaniah, and Zechariah) and sometimes also by the name of those for whom it is destined (as in Haggai and Malachi). These titles also declare that the content of the books in question, whether put in the mouth of God or in that of the prophet, is entirely the word of God. The remaining titles of the prophetic books indicate that they report the content of visions experienced by persons such as Isaiah, Amos, Obadiah, Nahum, and Habakkuk. The title of the book of Micah juxtaposes "the formula of the event of the word of the Lord" with the mention of a vision. In the context of the prophetic books the cause of the visions, though not stated explicitly, cannot be anything other than the Lord himself. He, therefore, is the author of the books in question.

The titles are not the only part of the prophetic books that declares them to be the Word of God; the numerous "prophetic formulae" that mark the text do the same. The most frequent expression, the "prophetic formula" par excellence, is "Thus says the Lord." By opening a discourse with this formula, the prophet presents himself as the messenger of the Lord. He informs his hearers that the discourse he addresses to them does not derive from him but has the Lord for its author.

Without pretending to be exhaustive, three other formulae which appear in the prophetic books should be noted: "oracle of the Lord," "says the Lord/God," and "the Lord speaks." Unlike the first expression, called the "messenger formula," which introduces the discourses, these latter conclude them. Acting as a signature affixed to the end of a document, they attest that the Lord is the author of the preceding discourse.

b) The Prophets: Messengers of the Lord

14. Four of the prophetic books narrate how the Lord ensured that their authors became his messengers: Isaiah (6:1-13), Jeremiah (1:4-10), Ezekiel (1:3–3:11), and Amos (7:15). The missions of Isaiah and Ezekiel are framed by a vision. The same is probably true for Jeremiah. The account of the mission of Isaiah is a good example of the genre, because it is quite developed but at the same time very succinct. In the divine council, in which Isaiah, in his vision, is present, the Lord, who is in search of a volunteer, says, "Whom shall I send, and who will go for us?" Isaiah responds: "Here I am; send me!" Accepting Isaiah's offer, the Lord concludes: "Go and say to this people. . . ." The message of the Lord follows (Isa 6:8-10). Punctuated by the verbs "send, go, say," the account concludes with the Lord's discourse, which Isaiah has the task of transmitting to the people. The same is true of the other three "accounts of prophetic sending" cited above, which also conclude with the order given by the Lord to his envoy to transmit the message that he communicates (Ezek 2:3-4; 3:4-11; Amos 7:15). In the account of the sending of Jeremiah the Lord insists on the peremptory character of his command (cf. also Amos 3:8) and, at the same time, on the accuracy that must mark the transmission of the message: "But the Lord said to me, 'Do not say, "I am only a boy"; for you shall go to all to whom I send you, and you shall speak whatever I command you'" (Jer 1:7; cf. 1:17; 26:2, 8; Deut 18:18, 20). These accounts establish the role of the messengers of the Lord which the prophetic books ascribe to their respective authors and consequently bear out the divine origin of their message.

2.2.2 The Historical Books: The Word of the Lord Has Infallible Efficacy and Calls to Conversion

a) The Books of Joshua–Kings

15. In the books of Joshua, Judges, Samuel, and Kings, which, according to Hebrew tradition, also belong to the prophetic collection, the Lord frequently speaks as in the prophetic books. In fact, at every stage of the conquest of the Promised Land, the Lord tells

Joshua what he must do. In Joshua 20:1-6 and 24:2-15 he addresses the people through Joshua, who thus fulfills the prophetic role. In the book of Judges, the Lord or his angel often speaks to leaders, above all to Gideon, or to the people. The Lord acts in person, except in Judges 4:6-7 and 6:7-9, when he makes use of the prophetess Deborah and an anonymous prophet to address Barak and all the people, respectively.

In the books of Samuel and Kings, however, with rare exceptions, the Lord addresses his hearers through prophetic figures. Their discourses, then, are framed by the same expressions that introduce, or recur in, the prophetic books. Among the books of the Bible, in fact, it is the books of Samuel and Kings that give the most attention to the prophets and to their activity as messengers of the Lord. In the greater part of the oracles reported in Samuel and Kings, the Lord announces the disasters that he will cause to fall upon the leaders of the people, especially on one or another king or his dynasty, or on the kingdoms of Israel (cf. 1 Kgs 14:15-16) and of Judah (cf. 2 Kgs 21:10-15), because they worship deities different from him. The divine announcements of misfortune are usually accompanied by the confirmation of their fulfillment. Samuel and Kings thus present themselves, in large part, as a succession of announcements of misfortune and their fulfillment. This succession ends only with the destruction of the kingdom of Judah. In the introduction to the accounts of the Babylonian Conquest (597–587 BC), 2 Kings 24:2 actually states that the destruction of Judah was the work of the Lord, who thus fulfilled what he had announced "by his servants the prophets." Since the Lord does not fail to accomplish what he announces, his word has an infallible efficacy. In other words, the Lord is the principal author of the history of his people; he announces its events and makes them happen.

As in the texts of which we have spoken, so also 2 Kings 17:7-20 synthesizes the history of Israel and Judah in a succession of discourses which the Lord addressed to them through "his servants the prophets." The tone of the discourses, however, is different. The Lord does not announce misfortunes to Israel and Judah but exhorts them to convert. Because they were obstinate in their refusal of the Lord's appeals (vv. 13-14), he ends up casting them far from his countenance.

b) The Books of Chronicles

16. As in Joshua–Kings, so also in Chronicles the discourses of the Lord abound. He speaks directly to Solomon (2 Chr 1:7, 11-12; 7:12-22). In general, the Lord addresses the king or the people through intermediaries; most of them receive a "prophetic" title, but there are those without titles. First place belongs to prophets such as Nathan (cf. 1 Chr 17:1-15). There are many others, but the Lord even uses seers such as Gad (cf. 1 Chr 21:9-12) and people who have various occupations and even foreign kings such as Neco (cf. 2 Chr 35:21) and Cyrus (cf. 2 Chr 36:23). The heads of the families of the temple musicians prophesy (cf. 1 Chr 25:1-3).

Chronicles takes up the concepts of the word of God expressed in Samuel and Kings. As in these books, but perhaps with less insistence, the discourses of the Lord have as their theme the announcement of events whose fulfillment has been established (cf. 1 Chr 11:1-3; 2 Chr 6:10; 10:15). Chronicles underlines this role of the word of the Lord in reference to the Babylonian Exile. According to 2 Chronicles 36:20-22, both the Exile and its end fulfill what the Lord announced through the mouth of Jeremiah (cf. Jer 25:11-14; 29:10). In terms that are different from 2 Kings 17:13-14, 2 Chronicles 36:15-16 picks up again the theme of the unremitting, if vain, attempts made by the Lord to keep his people from ruin by sending them messengers/prophets. Finally, it should be noted that Chronicles does not affirm the divine origin of the content of the books in question but, by making references to prophetic sources (cf. 2 Chr 36:12, 15-16, 21-22), appears to suggest it.

In short, the prophetic books present themselves entirely as the Word of the Lord. This idea occupies a predominant place in the historical books as well. Both groups, especially the historical books, specify that the Word of the Lord has an infallible efficacy and calls to conversion.

2.3 The Psalms

17. The Psalter is a collection of prayers that come from the personal and communal experience of the presence and action of the Lord. The Psalms express the prayer of Israel in the various epochs

of its history: in the period of the kings; then during the Exile, when God came to be recognized more and more as the king of Israel; and, finally, after the Exile up to the period of the Second Temple. Every psalm attests a strong and living relationship with God, and on this basis we can say that they come from God and are inspired by God. According to what the texts themselves show, one can observe, without claiming to be exhaustive, three types of relationship: (a) the experience of the intervention of God in the life of the believers; (b) the experience of the presence of God in the sanctuary; (c) the experience of God, source of all wisdom. These three types of relationship with God are lived on the basis of the Sinai covenant, which includes the promise of God's active presence in the daily life of the people and in the temple.

2.3.1 The Experience of God's Intervention in the Life of the Faithful

Those who pray experience the powerful help of God in two ways: as a response to their cry for help; as listening to the great wonders of God.

With regard to those praying as beneficiaries of God's help, we take from many possible examples the prayer of Psalm 30:8-13: "To you, O LORD, I cried, and to the LORD I made supplication: . . . Hear, O LORD, and be gracious to me! O LORD, be my helper! You have turned my mourning into dancing; you have taken off my sackcloth and clothed me with joy, so that my soul may praise you and not be silent. O LORD my God, I will give thanks to you forever."

An experience both personal and communal of the Lord who saves is the inspiring force of the psalms of supplication and praise. This experience is always at least recalled, if not narrated, at the beginning (e.g., Pss 18:5-7; 30:2) or end (e.g., Ps 142:6-8) or even in the middle part of the psalm (e.g., Pss 22:22; 85:7-9). Midway between the human word of supplication and that of praise stands the Word (which expresses the promise and action) of God (see Ps 30:12). Having perceived it, the psalmist feels inspired to recount it to others. Thus it is awaited, received, and praised not only by an individual but by all the people.

Those who pray attend to the wonders of the Lord since God speaks to them and to all the people through the great deeds which he has accomplished in the whole of creation and in Israel's history. Psalm 19:1-5 recalls the wonders of creation and describes their way of speaking: "The heavens are telling the glory of God, and the firmament proclaims his handiwork. Day to day pours forth speech, and night to night declares knowledge. There is no speech, nor are there words; their voice is not heard; yet their voice goes out through all the earth, and their words to the end of the world." It is the task of the one who prays to understand this language that speaks of the "glory of God" (cf. Ps 147:15-20) and express it with one's own words.

Psalm 105 tells of the works of God in the history of Israel and exhorts the individual and the people: "Remember the wonderful works he has done, his miracles, and the judgments he uttered" (v. 5). These "wonderful works he has done," recounted in the historical psalms, are also "the judgments he uttered." Although formulated by human beings in human terms, the words of this psalm are inspired by the Lord's mighty work. This voice of the Lord continues to resound in the here and now of the suppliant and of the people. It needs to be heeded.

2.3.2 The Experience of the Powerful Presence of God within the Sanctuary

18. Psalms 17 and 50 may be taken as examples. In the first text, the experience of God inspires a just man falsely accused to utter a prayer of unconditional trust in God; in the second, this experience makes God's voice heard as it denounces the erroneous behavior of the people.

The last verse of Psalm 17 expresses a certain hope: "As for me, I shall behold your face in righteousness; when I awake I shall be satisfied, beholding your likeness" (v. 15). Two other prayers of people who are persecuted end in a similar way. Psalm 11:7 concludes with the assertion, "The upright shall behold his face," and the penultimate verse of Psalm 27 says, "I believe that I shall see the goodness of the LORD in the land of the living" (v. 13; cf. vv. 4,

8, 9). The expression "the face of God" signifies God himself, the person of God according to his true and perfect reality. The expression "behold the face of God" signifies, then, an intense, real, and personal encounter with God, not through the organ of sight, but in the "vision" of faith. The unshakeable hope of having this experience of God ("I will behold," in the future) and the knowledge of God expressed in it are the source of the entire prayer.

Psalm 50 recounts the experience of a theophany in the temple liturgy. At the appearance of the God of the covenant (v. 5), the phenomena of Sinai are repeated, a devouring fire and a tempest (v. 3). The manifestation of the true reality of God and of his relationship with Israel ("I am God, your God!" v. 7) leads to an accusation against the people: "But now I rebuke you, and lay the charge before you" (v. 21). God criticizes his people's behavior in two ways: their relationship with God is focused exclusively on sacrifices (vv. 8-13), and their relationship with their neighbor is diametrically opposed to the commandments of the covenant (vv. 16-22). God asks that he be praised, invoked in distress (vv. 14-15, 23), and he expects righteousness toward one's neighbor (vv. 23).

Psalm 50, at the heart of the Psalter, recalls the prophetic forms; not only does it have the Lord speak, but it brings about that every supplication and every act of praise be interpreted as obedience to the divine command. The whole prayer is therefore "inspired" by God.

2.3.3 The Experience of God, Source of Wisdom

19. Wisdom and understanding are attributes of God (cf. Pss 136:5; 147:5). It is he who communicates them ("teach me wisdom in my secret heart"; Ps 51:6), making humans wise, capable, that is, of seeing all things as God sees them. David possessed such wisdom and understanding from the moment God called him to be king of Israel (cf. Ps 78:72).

The fear of God is the condition for being instructed by God and receiving wisdom. In the opening part of Psalm 25, the supplicant begs fervently for the Lord's instruction ("Make me know your ways, O LORD; teach me your paths. Lead me in your truth, and teach me"; vv. 4-5), relying on God's readiness to grant it

(vv. 8-9). The fear of God is the indispensable attitude for being beneficiaries of God's wisdom teaching: "Who are they that fear the LORD? He will teach them the way that they should choose" (Ps 25:12). Those who fear God receive not only the indication of the right way to follow but also, as Psalm 25 makes clear, a broader and deeper illumination: "The friendship of the LORD is for those who fear him, and he makes his covenant known to them" (v. 14); in other words, he grants them a relationship of intimate friendship and penetrating insight into the pact which he made with Israel on Sinai. The relationship with God, expressed with the terminology of the "fear of God," is clearly the source of inspiration from which so many wisdom psalms originate.

2.4 The Book of Sirach

20. In the prophetic books, it is God himself who speaks through the prophets. As we have seen, God addresses in various ways those whom he has chosen as his mouthpiece for the people of Israel. In the Psalms, it is the person who speaks to God, but this is done in his presence and by adopting forms of expression that presuppose an intimate communion with him. In the wisdom books, however, human beings speak to each other; yet the one who speaks and the one who listens are both deeply rooted in faith in the God of the people of Israel. Frequently in the Old Testament, wisdom is explicitly attributed to the Spirit of God (cf. Job 32:8; Wis 7:22; 9:17; also 1 Cor 12:4-11). Such books are called "wisdom books" because their authors explore and point out the ways of a human life guided by wisdom. In their search, they are conscious of the fact that wisdom is a gift of God, because "there is but one who is wise, greatly to be feared, seated upon his throne" (Sir 1:8). Wishing to illustrate precisely which modes of relationship with God are attested by these writings as a basis and source for what is taught by their authors, we have focused our research on the book of Sirach because of its concise character.

From the beginning, the author is aware that "All wisdom is from the Lord, and with him it remains forever" (Sir 1:1). Already in the prologue of the book, the translator indicates a way in which

God communicated wisdom to the author: "My grandfather Jesus," he writes, "who had devoted himself especially to the reading of the Law and the Prophets and the other books of our ancestors, and had acquired considerable proficiency in them, was himself also led to write something pertaining to instruction and wisdom." The careful and devout reading of the Sacred Scriptures, in which God speaks to the people of Israel, united the author with God, became the source of his wisdom, and led him to write his work. Thus one can clearly see a way in which the book comes from God.

What the translator affirms in the prologue is confirmed by the author himself in the heart of the book. After recounting wisdom's praise of herself (Sir 24:1-22), he identifies it with the writing of Moses: "All this is the book of the covenant of the Most High God, the law that Moses commanded us as an inheritance for the con-gregations of Jacob" (Sir 24:23). Sirach goes on to explain what the result of his study of the Law is and the purpose of his writing: "I will again make instruction shine forth like the dawn, and I will make it clear from far away. I will again pour out teaching like prophecy, and leave it to all future generations. Observe that I have not labored for myself alone, but for all who seek wisdom" (Sir 24:32-34; cf. 33:18). The wisdom that everyone, even in the future, can find in his writing is the fruit of his study of the Law and of what God taught him through the trials of life (cf. Sir 4:11, 17-18). He seems to offer a portrait of himself when he speaks of "the one who devotes himself to the study of the law of the Most High!" (38:34) and writes: "He seeks out the wisdom of all the ancients, and is concerned with prophecies" (39:1). He then indicates as a result: "If the great Lord is willing, he will be filled with the spirit of understanding; he will pour forth words of wisdom of his own and give thanks to the Lord in prayer" (Sir 39:6). The acquisition of wisdom as a fruit of study is recognized as a gift of God and leads to the prayer of praise. Everything, then, takes place in a living and continual union with God. The author asserts, not only for himself, but for all, that the fear of God and the observance of the Law give access to wisdom: "Whoever fears the Lord will do this, and who-ever holds to the law will obtain wisdom" (15:1).

In the last part of his work (44–50), Sirach concerns himself with the tradition of his people in a different way, praising the fathers and describing God acting through many people in history and in favor of Israel. With this review, he also shows how his own written work stems from the relationship with God. About Moses, in particular, he says: "He allowed him to hear his voice, and led him into the dark cloud, and gave him the commandments face to face, the law of life and knowledge, so that he might teach Jacob the covenant, and Israel his decrees" (45:5). He mentions many prophets, and in relation to Isaiah, he declares, "By his dauntless spirit he saw the future, and comforted the mourners in Zion" (48:24). Meditating on the Law and the Prophets, and hence listening to the Word of God, this wisdom author was in union with God, obtained wisdom, and acquired the elements for composing his work (see Sirach prologue).

In the concluding part, Sirach characterizes the content of his book as "instruction in understanding and knowledge" (50:27). He adds a beatitude: "Happy are those who concern themselves with these things, and those who lay them to heart will become wise. For if they put them into practice, they will be equal to anything, for the fear of the Lord is their path" (50:28-29). The beatitude requires meditation on and practice of the content of the book, and promises wisdom and the light of the Lord; all that is possible only if this written work comes from God.

2.5 Conclusion

21. Having finished the review of selected texts from the Old Testament, we can now look back at them from a synthetic perspective. The writings examined, although different as to date and place of composition, as well as to specific content and particular literary style, agree in presenting a single, great basic message: God speaks to us. The same unique God, in the multiplicity and variety of historical situations, seeks man and woman, reaches them, and speaks to them. And the message of God, different in form because of the concrete historical circumstances of revelation, constantly tends to promote a loving response in them. The writings that express this marvelous design of God are themselves permeated with God. Such

divine infusion renders them inspired and inspiring, capable, that is, of illuminating and encouraging the understanding and passion of believers. The reader perceives this and, trembling with wonder and joy, asks: what can this ineffable God who speaks to me give me? The authors of the New Testament, members of the people of Israel, know the "Scriptures" of their people and recognize them as an inspired word that comes from God. They show us how God continued speaking until he expressed his ultimate and definitive word in the sending of his Son (cf. Heb 1:1-2).

III. The Testimony of Select New Testament Texts

22. We have already noted as a characteristic of the New Testament writings that they show the relationship of their authors to God exclusively through the person of Jesus. The four gospels have a special place here. *Dei Verbum*, in fact, speaks of their "special pre-eminence, and rightly so, for they are the principal witness for the life and teaching of the incarnate Word, our Savior" (n. 18). We take into account, therefore, the privileged role of the gospels, which is why, after an introduction that explains what they have in common, we will set out first of all the particular approach of the Synoptic Gospels and then the approach characteristic of the Gospel of John. For the other types of New Testament writings, we will select the most important ones and will consider, therefore, the Acts of the Apostles, the letters of the Apostle Paul, the letter to the Hebrews, and Revelation.

3.1 The Four Gospels

23. The four gospels stand out from all the other books of Sacred Scripture insofar as they directly relate "all that Jesus did and taught" (Acts 1:1), and at the same time they show how Jesus prepared the missionaries who were to spread the Word of God revealed by him. Through their presentation of the person of Jesus and his relationship with God, and their presentation of the apostles with the formation and authority granted them by Jesus, the gospels witness the specific manner of their text's origin from God.

3.1.1 Jesus, Culmination of God's Revelation for All Peoples

The gospels manifest a real diversity among themselves in some details of the narrative and in certain theological orientations, but they also show significant convergence in their presentation of the person of Jesus and his message. Here we provide a synthesis, which underlines the principal points.

All four gospels present the person and story of Jesus as the culmination of the biblical story. Consequently, they frequently refer to the writings of the Old Testament, known especially in the Greek translation of the Septuagint but also in original Hebrew and Aramaic texts. Of great importance are the numerous connections which the gospels point out between Jesus and the patriarchs, Moses, and the prophets, as people whose memory and significance are embedded in the sacred writings of the Old Testament.

The gospels attest that Jesus is the fulfillment of the revelation of the God of Israel, of that God who calls, instructs, punishes, and often reconstitutes Israel as his own people, set apart from the other nations but destined to be a blessing for all peoples. At the same time, the gospels certainly broaden the universalism of the Old Testament and make it clear that in Jesus God addresses the whole human race of all times (cf. Matt 28:20; Mark 14:9; Luke 24:47; John 4:42).

The four gospels, each in its own way, assert that Jesus is the Son of God, not only as a messianic title, but also as an expression of a relationship—unique and unprecedented—with the heavenly Father, thus transcending the salvific and revelatory role of all other human beings. This is set out in the most explicit form in the Gospel of John, both at the beginning in the Prologue (1:1-18) and in the chapters on the risen Lord, first in the encounter with Thomas (20:28) and then in the final affirmation on the inexhaustible meaning of the life and teaching of Jesus (21:25). This same message is found in the Gospel of Mark in the form of a literary inclusion: at the beginning Jesus is declared to be the Christ and the Son of God (1:1), and at the end the testimony of the Roman centurion near the crucified Jesus is cited: "Truly this man was God's Son!" (15:39). The same content is attested by the other Synoptic Gospels in strong and explicit terms through a joyful prayer that Jesus addresses to

God his Father (Matt 11:25-27; Luke 10:21-22). Using truly unique expressions, Jesus not only announces the perfect equality and intimacy between God the Father and himself as the Son but also affirms that this relationship cannot be acknowledged except through an act of revelation: only the Son can reveal the Father, and only the Father can reveal the Son.

From a literary point of view, the gospels recount narrative episodes and didactic discourses, but, in reality, they basically transmit a story of revelation and salvation. They present the life of the incarnate Son of God, who, from the humble conditions of an ordinary life and through the cruel humiliations of his passion and death, reaches exaltation in glory. In this way, while communicating the revelation of God in his Son Jesus, the gospels implicitly indicate the provenance of their text from God.

3.1.2 The Presence and Formation of Eyewitnesses and Ministers of the Word

24. Every episode of the gospels is centered on Jesus, who is, however, always surrounded by his disciples. The term "disciples" refers to a group of Jesus' followers whose number is not specified. Every gospel speaks specifically of "the Twelve," a select group accompanying Jesus during his whole ministry, whose significance is of great importance. The Twelve form a community, precisely discernible from the personal names of its members. Each gospel relates that this group was chosen by Jesus (Matt 10:1-4; Mark 3:13-19; Luke 6:12-16; John 6:70); they followed him, becoming eyewitnesses of his ministry and taking on the role of plenipotentiary emissaries (Matt 10:5-8; Mark 3:14-15; 6:7; Luke 9:1-2; John 17:18; 20:21). Their number symbolizes the twelve tribes of Israel (Matt 19:28; Luke 22:30) and signifies the fullness of the people of God which must be reached through their mission to evangelize the whole world. Their ministry not only transmits the message of Jesus to all people in the future but also, in fulfillment of the prophecy of Isaiah on the coming of Emmanuel (7:14), perpetuates Christ's presence in history according to his promise: "And remember, I am with you always, to the end of the age" (Matt 28:20). The gospels,

in bearing witness to the special formation of the Twelve, manifest in a concrete way their own provenance from Jesus and from God.

3.2 The Synoptic Gospels

25. The Synoptic Gospels present the story of Jesus in a way that leaves no space between the perspective of the narrative's author and his portrayal of the person, life, and mission of Jesus. In describing Jesus' various relationships with God, the gospels implicitly indicate their own relationship with God, or their provenance from God, always through the person and the revelatory, salvific role of Jesus.

Only Luke provides an introduction to the two volumes of his work (Luke 1:1-4; cf. Acts 1:1), connecting his narrative with the previous stages of the apostolic tradition. He thus considers his work as standing within the stream of apostolic testimony about Jesus and the story of salvation, testimony that began with the first followers of Jesus ("eyewitnesses"), was proclaimed in the first apostolic preaching ("ministers of the word"), and is now continued in a new form by the Gospel of Luke. In this way, Luke explicitly points out his gospel's relationship with Jesus, revealer of God, and affirms the revelatory authority of his work.

At the center of each gospel we find the person of Jesus seen in his relationships with God, which are manifold and unique. These relationships manifest themselves in the events of Jesus' life and in his activity, but also in his role for salvation history. In an initial paragraph we will concern ourselves with the person and activity of Jesus, and in a second paragraph, with his role in the history of God with humanity.

3.2.1 Jesus and His Unique Relationship with God

26. The gospels illustrate Jesus' unique relationship with God in various ways. They present him as: (a) the Christ, the Son of God in his privileged and unique relationship with the Father; (b) one full of the Spirit of God; (c) the one who acts with the power of God; (d) one who teaches with the authority of God; (e) one whose relationship with God is definitively revealed and confirmed through his death and resurrection.

a) Jesus, Only Son of God the Father

Already in the infancy narratives of the gospels of Matthew and
Luke, there is a clear reference to the divine origin of Jesus (Matt
1:20; Luke 1:35) and to his unique relationship to the Father (Matt
2:15; Luke 2:49).

All three of the Synoptic Gospels go on to recount key events in
the life of Jesus in which he communicates directly with his Father;
and the Father, for his part, confirms the divine origin of his Son's
identity and mission.

In each Synoptic Gospel the public ministry of Jesus is preceded
by his baptism and a remarkable theophany. The heavens open, the
Spirit descends on Jesus, and the voice of God declares him to be
God's beloved Son (Matt 3:13-17; Mark 1:9-11; Luke 3:21-22).
After this inaugural event, the gospels recount that Jesus was driven
by the Spirit into the desert (Matt 4:1-11; Mark 1:12-13; Luke 4:1-
13) for a confrontation with Satan (Israel's sojourn in the desert is
thus evoked), and then his ministry begins in Galilee.

Another compelling theophany, the transfiguration of Jesus,
happens at the end of his Galilean ministry, when he sets out on his
journey toward Jerusalem, near the time of the Passover events. As
at the baptism, God the Father declares, "This is my Son, the Beloved" (Matt 17:5, par.) and explicitly underlines the authority that
belongs to him: "Listen to him!" Some elements of this theophany
evoke the Sinai event: the mountaintop, the presence of Moses and
Elijah, the dazzling transformation of the person of Jesus, and the
presence of the cloud that covers them with its shadow. In this way,
Jesus and his mission are connected with the revelation of God on
Sinai and with the history of the salvation of Israel.

Matthew's gospel contains a unique, revelatory title for Jesus.
In addition to his proper name, "Jesus," which he interprets with
the phrase "he will save his people from their sins" (Matt 1:21),
Matthew also has the title "Emmanuel" (1:23), which signifies
"God with us" (cf. Isa 7:14). In this way the Evangelist explicitly
affirms Jesus' embodiment of the divine presence and underscores
the teaching authority and the other actions of Jesus throughout
his ministry. The title "Emmanuel" reappears in a certain sense
in Matthew 18:20, where Jesus speaks of his presence within the

community ("For where two or three are gathered in my name, I am there among them"), and in 28:20 with the concluding promise of the risen Christ: "And remember, I am with you always, to the end of the age."

b) Jesus, Full of the Spirit of God

All the Synoptic Gospels refer to the descent of the Spirit of God upon Jesus on the occasion of his baptism (Matt 3:16; Mark 1:10; Luke 3:22) and reaffirm the action of the Holy Spirit in his deeds (cf. Matt 12:28; Mark 3:28-30). Luke, in particular, repeatedly mentions the Spirit that animates Jesus in his mission of teaching and healing (cf. Luke 4:1, 14, 18-21). The same Evangelist affirms that, in a moment of great emotion, Jesus "rejoiced in the Holy Spirit" (10:21) and said, "All things have been handed over to me by my Father; and no one knows who the Son is except the Father, or who the Father is except the Son" (Luke 10:21-22; cf. also Matt 11:25-27).

c) Jesus Acts with the Power of God

27. Jesus' unique relationship to God is also manifested in exorcisms and healings. In all three Synoptics, but especially in Mark, the exorcisms characterize the mission of Jesus. The power of God's Spirit present in Jesus is able to drive the evil spirit that seeks to destroy human beings (e.g., Mark 1:21-28). The clash with Satan that took place in the temptations at the beginning of his ministry continues during his life in the victorious combat against the evil forces that cause human suffering. The demonic powers themselves are presented as being agonizingly aware of Jesus' identity as Son of God (e.g., Mark 1:24; 3:11; 5:7). The "power" that comes from Jesus is the power of healing (cf. Mark 5:30). Such stories abound in all three Synoptic Gospels. When accused by his opponents of being empowered by Satan, Jesus replies with a summary statement that links his miraculous deeds to the power of the Holy Spirit, and the presence of the Kingdom of God: "But if it is by the Spirit of God that I cast out demons, then the kingdom of God has come to you" (Matt 12:28; cf. Luke 11:20).

The presence of the power of God in Jesus is disclosed in a special way in the episodes in which he manifests his authority even over the power of nature. The stories of the storm that is stilled and the walking on the water are equivalent to theophanies, in which Jesus exercises divine authority over the chaotic power of the sea and, when he walks on the waters, enunciates the divine name as his own (Matt 14:27; Mark 6:50). The disciples who witness the miracle in Matthew's account end up by confessing Jesus' identity as Son of God (Matt 14:33). The multiplication stories likewise reveal Jesus' unique power and authority (Matt 14:13-21; Mark 6:32-44; Luke 9:10-17; Matt 15:32-39; and Mark 8:1-10). These actions are linked to the divine gift of manna in the desert and to the prophetic ministries of Elijah and Elisha. At the same time, through the words and gestures over the loaves and the abundance of the leftover fragments, the eucharistic celebration of the Christian community, where the salvific power of Jesus unfolds sacramentally, is hinted at.

d) Jesus Teaches with the Authority of God

The Synoptic Gospels affirm that Jesus teaches with unique authority. At the Transfiguration, the voice from heaven explicitly demands: "This is my Son, the Beloved; listen to him!" (Mark 9:7; Matt 17:5; Luke 9:35). In the synagogue of Capernaum, the witnesses of the first teaching and first exorcism of Jesus exclaim: "What is this? A new teaching—with authority! He commands even the unclean spirits, and they obey him" (Mark 1:27). In Matthew 5:21-48, Jesus contrasts his teaching authoritatively with key points of the Law: "You have heard that it was said to those of ancient times. . . . But I say to you. . . ." He also declares that he is "lord of the sabbath" (Matt 12:8; Mark 2:28; Luke 6:5). The authority that he received from God extends to the forgiveness of sins (Matt 9:6; Mark 2:10; Luke 5:24).

e) The Death and Resurrection of Jesus as the Final Revelation and Confirmation of His Unique Relationship with God

28. The crucifixion of Jesus, an extremely cruel and ignominious fate, seems to confirm the opinion of his adversaries, who see him as

a blasphemer (Matt 26:65; Mark 14:63). They call on the crucified one to come down from the cross and to prove his assertion that he is the Son of God (Matt 27:41-43; Mark 15:31-32). Death on the cross seems to demonstrate that his actions and claims have been rejected by God. According to the gospels, however, Jesus, as he dies, expresses his most intimate union with God the Father, whose will he accepts (Matt 26:39, 42; Mark 14:36; Luke 22:42). And God the Father, by raising Jesus from the dead (Matt 28:6; Mark 16:6; Luke 24:6, 34), shows his complete and definitive approval of the person of Jesus in all his activities and claims. Whoever believes in the resurrection of Jesus crucified can no longer doubt his unique relationship with God the Father and the authenticity of his entire ministry.

3.2.2 Jesus and His Role in Salvation History

29. The Sacred Scriptures of the people of Israel are seen as an account of the ways God deals with this people and as the Word of God. The Synoptic Gospels demonstrate Jesus' relationship with God, also by characterizing his story as the fulfillment of the Scriptures. Moreover, Jesus' particular relationship with God is also shown in his self-manifestation at the end of time.

a) The Fulfillment of the Scriptures

It is important to note that Jesus not only perfects the teaching of Moses and the prophets with what he says, but in addition presents himself as the personal fulfillment of the Scriptures. Matthew observes in 2:15 that from childhood Jesus repeats Israel's journey "out of Egypt" (cf. Hos 11:1). Filled with the Holy Spirit (Luke 4:15), and having read Isaiah in the synagogue of Nazareth, he closes the book and declares, "Today this scripture has been fulfilled in your hearing" (4:16-21). Similarly, he sends word to John in prison that what the Baptist's own envoys see comprehensively fulfills the messianic prophecies of Isaiah (Matt 11:2-6, linking Isa 26:19; 29:18-19; 35:5; 61:1). The programmatic beginning of the Gospel of Mark provides, in the initial verses, a summary of Jesus' identity, not only in the first line where it speaks of "Jesus Christ, the Son of God" (1:1), but also in the verses that follow which announce the

Lord himself, whose advent is prepared according to the testimony of the prophets (1:2-3, in reference to Exod 23:20; Mal 3:1; Isa 40:3). If the Evangelists present him coherently as a descendant of David, he is also said to be greater than Solomon in wisdom (Matt 12:42; Luke 11:31), greater than the temple (Matt 12:6), or greater than Jonah (Matt 12:41; Luke 11:32). In the Sermon on the Mount, he legislates with an authority which transcends that of Moses (cf. Matt 5:21, 27, 33, 38, 43).

b) The Fulfillment of History in the Triumphal Return of Jesus

According to the Synoptic Gospels, the strict relationship of Jesus with God is manifested not only in the fact that the life of Jesus is the fulfillment of the history of God with Israel but also in the other fact that the whole of history is brought to its fulfillment through Jesus' return in glory. In the apocalyptic discourses (Matt 24–25; Mark 13; Luke 21), he prepares his disciples for the travails of history after his death and resurrection and exhorts them to be faithful and watchful for his return. They live in an intermediate period between the fulfillment of earlier history, brought about by the work and life of Jesus, and its definitive fulfillment at the end of all time. This is the time of the communities that believe in Jesus, the time of the Church. In this intermediate period, Christians have the assurance that the risen Lord is always with them (Matt 28:20), also through the power of the Holy Spirit (Luke 24:49; cf. Acts 1:8). They also have the duty of announcing the Gospel of Jesus to all peoples (Matt 26:13; Mark 13:10; Luke 24:47), of making them disciples of Jesus (Matt 28:19), following Jesus in their lives. Their whole life and all this time unfolds against the backdrop of the fulfillment of history that will come about with the triumphant return of Jesus.

3.2.3 Conclusion

30. The Synoptic Gospels show Jesus' unique relationship to God in all his life and activity; they also show the unique meaning of Jesus for the fulfillment of the history of God with the people of Israel and for the definitive fulfillment of all history. It is in Jesus that God reveals himself and his plan of salvation for all humanity; it is

in Jesus that God speaks to human beings; it is through Jesus that they are brought to God and united with him; and it is through Jesus that they obtain salvation. Through their presentation of Jesus, the Word of God, the gospels themselves become the word of God. It is the nature of the Sacred Scriptures of Israel to speak authoritatively of God and to lead with assurance to God. The same trait appears in the gospels, and leads to the formation of a canon of Christian writings linked to the canon of the Hebrew Sacred Scriptures.

3.3 The Gospel of John

31. The prologue of the Gospel of John closes with a solemn affirmation: "No one has ever seen God. It is God the only Son, who is close to the Father's heart, who has made him known" (1:18). This presentation of the nature of Jesus (only-begotten Son, God, intimate union with the Father) and of his unique capacity to know and reveal God not only is attested at the beginning of the gospel but, being a fundamental assumption, is confirmed by the whole Johannine work. Whoever enters into a relationship with Jesus and is open to his word receives from him the revelation of God the Father. In common with the other gospels, the Fourth Gospel insists on the fulfillment of the Scriptures through the work of Jesus and thus affirms its being part of God's salvific plan. But a characteristic of the Gospel of John is that it points out some special qualities of the Evangelist's relationship with Jesus, in particular: (a) the contemplation of the glory of the only-begotten Son; (b) explicit eyewitness testimony; (c) the instruction of the Spirit of truth for the witnesses. These specific characteristics, which connect the Evangelist more intimately with the person of Jesus, have the effect of showing the provenance of his gospel from God himself. We will expand here on these special characteristics.

3.3.1 Contemplating the Glory of the Only-Begotten Son

The prologue says: "And the Word became flesh and lived among us, and we have seen his glory, the glory as of a father's only son, full of grace and truth" (1:14). Having affirmed the incarnation of the Word and his insertion into humanity as a definitive dwelling place of the God of the covenant, the text speaks right away of a deep personal encounter with the incarnate Word. In the Johannine texts, "to contemplate" signifies not a momentary, superficial act of seeing but an intense and lasting perception, together with reflection, and a growing understanding and adherence in faith. In John 11:45, the direct object of contemplation is indicated as "what he did," that is, the raising of Lazarus from the dead, and faith in Jesus is mentioned as a consequence. In John 1:14b, the fruit of contemplation, that is, believing comprehension, is indicated as the only-begotten Son who comes from the Father (cf. 1 John 1:1; 4:14). The immediate object of contemplation, therefore, is Jesus, his person and activity, since the Word of God made himself visible to human beings during his life on earth.

The author includes himself in a group ("we") of attentive witnesses who, having contemplated the deeds of Jesus, came to faith in him as the only-begotten Son of God the Father. The Evangelist's writings are grounded on his being an eyewitness and on his faith in Jesus as Son of God; it follows indirectly that this written work comes from Jesus and therefore from God. We repeat that John is part of a group of believing witnesses. The first conclusion of the Fourth Gospel (20:30-31) allows us to identify this group. The Evangelist speaks explicitly of his work ("this book") and of the "signs" narrated there and says that Jesus performed them "in the presence of his disciples." These latter turn out to be the group of eyewitnesses to which the author of the Fourth Gospel belongs.

3.3.2 Explicit Eyewitness Testimony

32. On two occasions the Evangelist explicitly underlines that he was an eyewitness of what he writes. At the end of the gospel, we read, "This is the disciple who is testifying to these things and has written them, and we know that his testimony is true" (21:24). A group ("we") presents the disciple—identified with the protagonist of the final narrative—as a trustworthy witness and as the writer of the whole work. This is the disciple whom Jesus loved (21:20), who, because of his particular closeness to Jesus, was a witness of

his activity on other occasions too (13:23; 19:26; 20:2; 21:7). This confirms how this gospel comes from Jesus and from God. Those who declare, "we know," express their awareness of being qualified to make such a judgment. This constitutes an act of recognition, reception, and recommendation of the written work on the part of the believing community.

In another passage, the eyewitness testimony is made explicit by the outpouring of water and blood after the death of Jesus: "He who saw this has testified so that you also may believe. His testimony is true, and he knows that he tells the truth" (19:35). The concepts of vision, testimony, truth, and belief are decisive. The eyewitness asserts the truth of the testimony with which he addresses himself to a community ("you"), exhorting it to share his faith (cf. 20:31; 1 John 1:1-3). This faith concerns not only the events that have taken place but also their meaning, which is expressed in two Old Testament citations (cf. 19:36-37). From the context, we know that the eyewitness is the Beloved Disciple who stood by the cross of Jesus and who was addressed by Jesus (19:25-27). In John 19:35, therefore, the writer highlights, with particular reference to the death of Jesus, what John 21:24 states in relation to all the things recounted in the Fourth Gospel: this was written by an author who, by direct experience and by faith, was intimately united to Jesus and to God and who communicates his testimony to a community of believers who share the same faith.

3.3.3 The Teaching of the Spirit of Truth for the Witnesses

33. The testimony of the disciple is made possible by the gift of the Holy Spirit. In his farewell discourse (John 14–16), Jesus says to the disciples: "When the Advocate comes, whom I will send to you from the Father, the Spirit of truth who comes from the Father, he will testify on my behalf. You also are to testify because you have been with me from the beginning" (15:26-27). The disciples are eyewitnesses of Jesus' activity "from the beginning." But the testimony of faith, that which leads to belief in Jesus as Christ and Son of God (cf. 20:31), is given by the power of the Spirit, who, proceeding from the Father and sent by Jesus, creates in the disciples

the most vibrant union with God. The world cannot receive the Spirit (14:17), but the disciples receive it for their mission in the world (17:18). Jesus specifies how the Spirit witnesses to him: he "will teach you everything, and remind you of all that I have said to you" (14:26) and "will guide you into all the truth" (16:13). The work of the Spirit refers entirely to the activity of Jesus, and it has the task of leading to an ever deeper understanding of the truth, that is, of Jesus' revelation of God the Father (cf. 1:17-18). Each disciple's testimony about Jesus becomes effective only through the action of the Holy Spirit. The same holds for the Fourth Gospel, which presents itself as the written testimony of the disciple loved by Jesus.

3.4 The Acts of the Apostles

34. Not only is the gospel attributed to Luke, but also the book of the Acts of the Apostles (cf. Luke 1:1-4; Acts 1:1). Luke explicitly indicates that the source of his gospel was "those who from the beginning were eyewitnesses and ministers of the word" (Luke 1:2), suggesting, in this way, that his gospel comes from Jesus, the ultimate and supreme revealer of God the Father. He does not present the source of the book of Acts and its divine provenance in the same explicit way. It should be noted, however, that, on the one hand, the names in the list of apostles are identical in Acts 1:13 and Luke 6:14-16 (except for Judas), and, on the other, that in Acts their character as eyewitnesses (Acts 1:21-22; 10:40-41) and their task of being ministers of the word (Acts 6:2; cf. 2:42) are highlighted. In Acts, then, Luke describes the activity of those of whom he speaks in Luke 1:2, who constitute, therefore, the source for both his works.

We can presume that Luke informed himself about their activity (the theme of the book of Acts) with the same care (cf. Luke 1:3) with which, through them, he carried out his inquiry about the activities of Jesus.

The basic contribution for the divine provenance of the book of Acts is the immediate, personal relationship of these "eyewitnesses and ministers of the word" with Jesus. Their relationship to Jesus is seen particularly in their discourses and actions, in the working of the Holy Spirit, and in the interpretation of the Sacred Scriptures.

We will now set out in concrete terms these various elements that attest the provenance of the book of Acts from Jesus and from God.

3.4.1 The Apostles' Direct, Personal Relationship with Jesus

The book of Acts recounts the proclamation of the Gospel by the apostles, especially Peter, and by Paul. At the beginning of the book, Luke presents the list of apostles, comprising Peter and the other ten (Acts 1:13). These eleven are the nucleus of the community to which the risen Lord manifests himself (cf. Luke 24:9, 33), and they constitute an essential bridge between the Gospel of Luke and the book of Acts (cf. Acts 1:13, 26).

The identity of the names in the list of Luke 6:14-16 and in that of Acts 1:13 draw attention to the long and intense personal relationship of each of the apostles with Jesus. This was their privilege during the ministry of Jesus, and it made them protagonists of the book of Acts. These apostles (Acts 1:2) also share conversation and meals with Jesus before his ascension (Acts 1:3-4). To them he promised "the power of the Holy Spirit," designating them to be his witnesses "to the ends of the earth" (Acts 1:8). All of these details favor the acceptance of the narrative of Acts as coming from Jesus and from God.

Paul, the protagonist of the second part of Acts, is also characterized by his direct, personal relationship with Jesus. His encounter with the risen Lord is recounted and highlighted three times (Acts 9:1-22; 22:3-16; 26:12-18). Paul himself clearly affirms the divine origin of his gospel: "For I did not receive it from a human source, nor was I taught it, but I received it through a revelation of Jesus Christ" (Gal 1:12). The "we" sections of the book (Acts 16:10-18; 20:5-15; 21:1-18; 27:1–28:16) evoke the relationship of the book's author with Paul and, through Paul, with Jesus.

3.4.2 The Discourses and Deeds of the Apostles

35. The activity of the apostles, recounted in the book of Acts, manifests their varied relationship with Jesus.

The discourses of Peter (Acts 1:15-22; 2:14-36; 3:12-26; 10:34-43) and Paul (e.g., Acts 13:16-41) are significant summaries of the life and ministry of Jesus. They present the fundamental information about him: his Davidic descent (13:22-23), his connection with Nazareth (2:22; 4:10), his ministry beginning in Galilee (10:37-39). Special emphasis is given to his passion and death, involving the Jews (2:23; 3:13; 4:10-11) and the pagans (2:23; 4:26-27), Pilate (3:13; 4:27; 13:28) and Herod (4:27); it is also given to the suffering of the cross (5:30; 10:39; 13:29), the burial (13:29), and the resurrection by God (2:24, 32; etc.).

In the presentation of the resurrection of Jesus, the Father's activity is emphasized as opposed to human activity: "You crucified and killed [him]. . . . But God raised him up, having freed him from death" (2:23-24; cf. 3:15; etc.). God raised Jesus up to his right hand (2:33; 5:31) and glorified him (3:13). The emphasis, therefore, is on the very close relationship of Jesus with God and at the same time on the divine origin of what is narrated. The Christological titles of the Gospel of Luke are found also in the book of Acts: Christ (2:31; 3:18), Lord (2:36; 11:20), Son of God (9:20; 13:33), Savior (5:31; 13:23). In general, God is the source of these titles, through which is expressed the nature and assignment he bestowed on Jesus (cf. 2:36; 5:31; 13:33).

The miraculous deeds also link the apostles to Jesus. Jesus' miracles were signs of the Kingdom of God (Luke 4:18; 11:20; cf. Acts 2:22; 10:38). He entrusted this task to the Twelve (Luke 9:1). The book of Acts mentions in a general way "wonders and signs" (2:43; 5:12; 14:3) as works of the apostles. It also recounts individual miracles, such as healings (3:1-10; 5:14-16; 14:8-10), exorcisms (5:16; 8:7; 19:12), raising from the dead (9:36-42; 20:9-10). The apostles perform these deeds in the name of Jesus, with his power and authority (3:1-10; 9:32-35).

The activity of the apostles is totally determined by Jesus; it comes from him and leads back to him and to God the Father. Acts also highlights the continuity of the divine plan, fulfilled in Jesus Christ and then continued in the Church. In the miracles, in particular, Luke sees the divine confirmation of the apostolic mission, as happened for the mission of Moses (7:35-36) and of Jesus himself (2:22).

3.4.3 The Work of the Holy Spirit

36. The relationship of the apostles with Jesus is also demonstrated by means of the Holy Spirit that Jesus promised and sent to them and in which they accomplish their works.

To them the risen Lord announces "the promise of the Father" (Acts 1:4; cf. Luke 24:49), baptism "with the Holy Spirit" (Acts 1:5), "the power" of the Holy Spirit (Acts 1:8). On the day of Pentecost the Holy Spirit descends on them, and "all of them were filled with the Holy Spirit" (Acts 2:4), promised by the Father and poured out by Jesus now exalted at the right hand of God (Acts 2:33). In this Spirit, "Peter, standing with the Eleven" (Acts 2:14), gives with vigor the first public testimony to the work and the resurrection of Jesus (Acts 2:14-41).

In the brief description of the life of the Jerusalem Church, the apostolic activity is summed up in these terms: "With great power the apostles gave their testimony to the resurrection of the Lord Jesus" (4:33; cf. 1:22; etc.), and this testimony takes place under the influence of the Spirit (4:8, 31; etc.). The ministry of Paul, who proclaims the resurrection of Jesus (13:30, 37) and is filled with the Holy Spirit (cf. 9:17; 13:2, 4, 9) is described in identical terms.

3.4.4 The Fulfillment of the Old Testament

37. The Gospel of Luke recounts how the risen Lord explained the Sacred Scriptures to his disciples, guiding them to understand that in his passion, death, and resurrection, God's salvific plan, announced beforehand by Moses, the prophets, and the Psalms (Luke 24:27, 44), was accomplished. In the book of Acts there are about thirty-seven citations from the Old Testament, most of which occur in speeches that Peter, Stephen, and Paul direct to Jewish audiences. References to divinely inspired texts, showing their fulfillment in Jesus, give the words of the Christian preachers an analogous value.

The Christological events that make up the content of the preaching as well as the concomitant facts are linked to the Scriptures. In the opening discourse of Pentecost, Peter explains the occurrence of extraordinary phenomena caused by the coming of the Spirit in light of the prophecy of Joel 3:1-5 (Acts 2:4-13, 15). At the end of the book Paul interprets the Roman Jews' rejection of his message (Acts 28:23-25) by going back to the prophecy of Isaiah 6:9-10. What happens at the beginning and the end of the apostolic mission is linked to the prophetic Word of God. This kind of inclusion can suggest the idea that all that happens and is recounted in this book corresponds to the salvific plan of God.

Regarding the content of the apostolic preaching, we limit ourselves to a few examples. Peter confirms the proclamation of the resurrection of Jesus (2:24) by citing Psalm 16:8-11, attributed to David (2:29-32). He uses Psalm 110:1, also attributed to David, to establish the exaltation of Jesus to God's right hand (2:33). There are also comprehensive references to all the prophets, through whom God foretold the destiny of Jesus (cf. 3:18, 24; 24:14; 26:22; 28:23). Citing Psalm 2:7 (Acts 13:32-33) Paul presents the resurrection of Jesus as the fulfillment of the promise made to the fathers.

The book of Acts attests in a special way how the primitive Church not only received the Hebrew Scriptures as its own inheritance but also appropriated the vocabulary and theology of inspiration, as is evident from the way it cites Old Testament texts. Thus, at both the beginning (Acts 1:16) and the end of the book (Acts 28:15), the Holy Spirit is stated to speak through the authors and the biblical texts. At the beginning, the Scriptures, declared fulfilled by Jesus, are characterized as that "which the Holy Spirit through David foretold" (1:16; cf. also 4:25), and, at the end, the words of Paul, which bring the two volumes of Luke's work to a close, cite Isaiah 6:9-10 in similar terms: "The Holy Spirit was right in saying to your ancestors through the prophet Isaiah" (28:25). This way of referring to the Holy Spirit, who speaks in the biblical language, using human authors as intermediaries, is the model taken up by the Christians, not only to describe the inspired Hebrew Scriptures, but also to characterize the apostolic preaching. Acts, in fact, presents the preaching of the Christian missionaries, in particular that of Peter (4:8) and Paul (13:9), in a way that is analogous to the prophetic discourse of the Old Testament and to the ministry of Jesus: they are verbal expressions (more in oral than in written form) that come from the fullness of the Spirit.

3.4.5 Conclusion

38. It is characteristic of the book of Acts that it recounts the activity of the "eyewitnesses and ministers of the word," who had a multifaceted relationship with Jesus. They are, above all, witnesses of Jesus' resurrection, which they attest on the basis of encounters with the risen Lord and in the power of the Holy Spirit. They present the story of Jesus as the fulfillment of the salvific plan of God, referring to the Old Testament, and they see their own activity in the same light. Everything that is recounted comes from Jesus and from God. Through this clear feature of the theme of the book of Acts, the text also comes from Jesus and from God.

3.5 The Letters of the Apostle Paul

39. Paul attests the divine provenance of the Scriptures of Israel, of his gospel, of his apostolic ministry, and of his letters.

3.5.1 Paul's Witness to the Divine Origin of the Scriptures

Paul unambiguously recognizes the authority of the Scriptures, bears witness to their divine origin, and sees them as prophecies of the Gospel. He designates as Sacred Scripture (cf. Rom 1:2) the books received by the Jewish tradition in the Greek language. Their truth and inspiration are never called into question. As a believing Hebrew, he receives them as witnesses of the will and salvific plan of God for humanity. Along with his coreligionists, he believes in their truth, in their sanctity, and in their unity. Through them, God communicates with us, questions us, and makes his will known to us (Rom 4:23-25; 15:4; 2 Cor 9:10; 10:4, 11).

It should be added straightaway that Paul reads and accepts the Scriptures as prophecies of Christ and of our times (Rom 16:25-26); in other words, as prophecies of a salvation offered in and through Jesus Christ, and therefore as prophecies of the Gospel (Rom 1:2). They are Christologically directed and should be read as such (2 Cor 3).

As word of God and testimony in favor of the Gospel, the Scriptures confirm the unity and stability of the salvific plan of God, which has been the same from the beginning (Rom 9:6-29).

3.5.2 Paul Attests the Divine Origin of His Gospel

40. In the first chapter of his letter to the Galatians, Paul admits that, because of his zeal for the Law, he had persecuted the Church, but he confesses that God, in his infinite goodness, revealed his Son to him (Gal 1:16; cf. Eph 3:1-6). Through this revelation, Jesus of Nazareth, whom Paul had previously seen as a blasphemer, a pseudo-messiah, became the Risen One, the glorious Messiah, conqueror of death, the Son of God. In the same letter (Gal 1:12), he declares that his gospel was revealed to him, and by "gospel" we should understand the principal components of the journey and mission of Jesus, at least his salvific death and resurrection.

In Galatians 1–2 Paul goes on to announce that his gospel does not include circumcision. In other words, he declares that, according to what has been revealed to him, it is not necessary to have oneself circumcised and become a subject of the Mosaic Law to inherit the eschatological promises. For Paul, to subject Christians of non-Hebrew origin to circumcision was not a peripheral or transient question but touches the heart of the Gospel. In fact, he firmly declares that those who have had themselves circumcised—to become subject to the Mosaic Law and to obtain righteousness through it—make Christ's death on the cross meaningless for themselves: "I, Paul, am telling you that if you let yourselves be circumcised, Christ will be of no benefit to you" (Gal 5:2; cf. 5:4; 2:21). What is at stake, therefore, is the Gospel itself, a Gospel that was revealed to him and that, consequently, cannot be modified.

How does Paul show in Galatians 1–2 that his gospel, in which circumcision plays no part, is of divine origin? He begins by saying that such a rendering of the Gospel could not come from himself, since when he was a Pharisee he was fiercely opposed to it, and because, if he is now proclaiming the opposite of what he thought earlier, it is not because of intellectual volatility: all his coreligionists knew well, in fact, that he was firm in his convictions (Gal 1:13-14). Paul goes on to show that his gospel cannot come from the other apostles, not only because he visited them long after his encounter with Christ, but also because he did not hesitate to contradict Peter, the best-known of the apostles, when he effectively made circumcision a discriminating factor among Christians (Gal 2:11-14). Finally, since his gospel was revealed to him, he too had to be obedient to what God had made known to him. That is why he can say at the beginning of the same letter to the Galatians, "But even if we or an angel from heaven should proclaim to you a gospel contrary to what we proclaimed to you, let that one be accursed!" (Gal 1:8; cf. 1:9). Why did Paul want to emphasize the revealed nature of his gospel? Such a divine origin was, in fact, contested by the Judaizing missionaries, since circumcision was imposed by a clear divine oracle of the Mosaic law (Gen 17:10-14). Now, Genesis 17:10-14 affirms that, to obtain salvation, it is necessary to belong to the family of Abraham and, therefore, to be circumcised. In two of his letters, Galatians and Romans, Paul has to demonstrate that his gospel does not go against the Scriptures and does not contradict Genesis 17:10-14, a passage that does not admit exceptions. Paul cannot, in fact, declare that this oracle is no longer valid, since it is recognized as obligatory by all observant Jews. Unable to do without it, Paul must interpret it differently, but he cannot do so without appealing to other scriptural passages (Gen 1:6 and Ps 32:1-2 in Rom 4:3, 6), which constitute the basis on which Genesis 17:10-14 needs to be interpreted.

3.5.3 Paul's Apostolic Ministry and Its Divine Origin

41. Paul also had to insist on the divine origin of his apostolate, because some in the group of the apostles denigrated it and minimized the value of his gospel. Even if he had encountered the Risen One, he was not part of the group of those who lived with Jesus and were witnesses of his teaching, miracles, and passion. That is why he insists on the fact that he was set apart and called by the Lord to be an apostle to the Gentiles (Rom 1:5; 1 Cor 1:1; 2 Cor 1:1; Gal 1:1). That is also why, in the long eulogy he makes of himself in 2 Corinthians 10–13, he mentions revelations he received from the Lord (2 Cor 12:1-4). This is not a rhetorical exaggeration or a pious lie to display his own status as an apostle but a simple recognition of the truth. In his self-commendation in 2 Corinthians 10–13, Paul insists much less on the exceptional revelations of which he was the recipient and puts greater emphasis on an apostle's sufferings for the churches, because the power of God is made fully known

through his weaknesses. In other words, when he makes known the revelations received from God, Paul does so not in order to be admired by the churches but to show how the qualities of the authentic apostolate are rather labor and sufferings. His testimony, therefore, is worthy of trust.

Paul also notes in Galatians 2:7-9 that when he went to Jerusalem James, Peter, and John, the most authoritative and influential among the apostles, recognized that God had constituted him as apostle to the Gentiles. Paul, therefore, is not the only person to assert the divine origin of his vocation, since it was recognized by the ecclesiastical authorities of the time.

3.5.4 Paul Attests the Divine Origin of His Letters

42. Paul does not only declare the divine origin of his apostolate and of his gospel. The fact that his gospel was revealed to him does not automatically guarantee the accuracy and reliability of its transmission. That is why right at the beginning of his letters he recalls his call and apostolic mandate; in Romans 1:1, for example, he defines himself thus: "Paul, a servant of Jesus Christ, called to be an apostle, set apart for the gospel of God." He holds that his letters faithfully transmit his gospel and wants them to be read in all the churches (cf. Col 4:16).

Even the disciplinary directives that are not directly linked to the Gospel must be received by the faithful of the various churches as if they were a command of the Lord (1 Cor 7:17b; 14:37). Certainly Paul does not ascribe an equal authority to all of his pronouncements, as his argumentation relating to specific cases in 1 Corinthians 7 shows, but, because they often explain and justify his gospel, his arguments (cf. Rom 1–11 and Gal 1–4) present themselves somehow as a new and authoritative interpretation of the Gospel itself.

3.6 The Letter to the Hebrews

43. The author of the letter to the Hebrews does not make any claim to apostolic authority, unlike Paul, who claims to have received

the Gospel directly from Christ (Gal 1:1, 12, 16). There are, however, two passages of exceptional importance in this regard: 1:1-2,
where the author gives a summary of the history of God's revelation
to human beings and shows the strict connection between the two
Testaments as regards divine revelation, and 2:1-4, where he presents
himself as belonging to the second Christian generation, as one who
received the word of God, the message of salvation, not directly
from the Lord Jesus, but through the witnesses of Christ, from the
disciples who listened to him.

3.6.1 The History of God's Revelation

At the beginning of his text, the author observes: "Long ago God
spoke to our ancestors in many and various ways by the prophets,
but in these last days he has spoken to us by a Son" (Heb 1:1-2). In
this admirable opening phrase, the author outlines the whole history of the Word of God addressed to humanity. The passage is of
singular importance for the theme of revelation and inspiration and
merits a careful explanation.

An important fact is solemnly affirmed here: God sought to
enter into a personal relationship with human beings. He himself
took the initiative in this encounter: *God spoke.* The verb used does
not have a direct object; the content of this word is not specified.
Instead, the persons put in relationship are named: God, the fathers,
the prophets, us, the Son. The Word of God is presented here not
as a revelation of the truth but as a means of establishing relations
between persons.

In the history of the Word of God, there are two principal stages.
The repetition of the same verb, "to speak," expresses a clear continuity, and the parallelism of the two phrases highlights the similarity
of the two interventions. But the differences mark out the diversity
in epoch, manner, audience, and mediators.

With regard to epochs, the first, simply chronological ("in ancient times"), stands in contrast to another more complex one. The
author resorts to a biblical expression, "in these last days," which
vaguely indicated the future (cf. Gen 49:1) but was specified when
applied to the era of the definitive divine intervention "in the lat-

ter days" (Ezek 38:16; Dan 2:28; 10:14). The author makes use of the same formula but adds a new specification: "in these days" (in which we are living). Materially, this is a minute revision, but one that manifests a radical change of perspective. In the Old Testament, God's decisive intervention was always situated in the obscurity of the future. Here the author asserts that the final age is already present, because a new era has been inaugurated by the death and resurrection of Christ (Acts 2:17; 1 Cor 10:11; 1 Pet 1:20). If "these days" are part of the final era, the last day has not yet arrived (cf. John 6:39; 12:48); it is only drawing near (Heb 10:25). But from now on, Christian existence participates in the definitive benefits promised for the latter days (6:4-5; 12:22-24, 28). God's relationship with humanity now stands on another level; it has passed from promise to realization, from prefiguration to fulfillment. The difference is qualitative.

The way in which the Word of God is presented is not the same in the two periods of the history of salvation. In ancient times, it was characterized by multiplicity: "many times" (or more literally, "in many parts," "in a fragmentary way") and "in many ways." There is richness in this multiplicity. God untiringly (cf. Jer 7:13) found ways to reach us: giving orders, making promises, punishing rebels, comforting the suffering, and using all forms of possible expressions, such as awesome theophanies, consoling visions, brief oracles or grand panoramas of history, preaching of the prophets, songs and liturgical rites, laws, stories. But multiplicity is also an indication of imperfection (cf. Heb 7:23; 10:1-2, 11-14). God is expressing himself partially. Like a good teacher, he began by stating the elementary things in the most accessible way. He spoke of inheritance and of land, he promised and achieved the liberation of his people, and he granted them temporary institutions: a royal dynasty, a hereditary priesthood. But all this was nothing but a prefiguration. In the final phase, the Word of God was given completely, in a definitive and perfect way. The dispersed riches of earlier times were reunited and brought to their culmination in the unity of the mystery of Christ.

A change in the word's audience corresponds to the succession of time periods. The word of ancient times was addressed "to the fathers," broadly speaking, that is, to all the generations that received the prophetic message (cf. 3:9). The definitive word was addressed to "us." The pronoun "us" includes the authors and those for whom the text was destined, and also the witnesses who heard Christ (cf. 2:3) and their contemporaries.

When speaking of mediators, the author uses a curious, uncommon expression: God spoke "in" the prophets, "in" the Son; normally one says, "through" (Matt 1:22; 2:15; etc.; Acts 28:25). The author may have had in mind the presence of God himself active in his messengers. It is the only meaning that suits the second expression: "in the Son." The prophets in a broad sense, those whose interventions the Bible reports to us, are succeeded by a final messenger who is "Son." The position chosen for his name—at the end of the phrase—focuses attention on him. Once he is named, nothing is said except in relation to him (Heb 1:2-4). God's encounter with humans comes about only in him. God first sent "his servants the prophets" (Jer 7:25; 25:4; 35:15; 44:4). Now his messenger is no longer a mere servant; he is "the Son." Speaking through the prophets, God let himself be known, but indirectly, through an agent; now the encounter with the Word of God is realized in the Son. No longer is it a man differing from God who speaks to us, but a divine person, whose unity with the Father is expressed with the strongest formulae that the author could find: "the reflection of God's glory and the exact imprint of God's very being" (Heb 1:3). It was not enough for God to address himself to us by taking up our language; he came, in the person of Jesus Christ, to share our existence in a real way and to speak not only the language of words but also that of a life offered up and of bloodshed.

3.6.2 The Author's Relationship to the Revelation of the Son

44. After treating one aspect of his teaching, the Word of God addressed to humanity in the prophets and in the Son (1:1-14), the author immediately specifies its connection with life and points out his own relationship to the Son: "Therefore we must pay greater attention to what we have heard, so that we do not drift away from it. For if the message declared through angels was valid, and every transgression or disobedience received a just penalty, how can we

escape if we neglect so great a salvation? It was declared at first through the Lord, and was attested to us by those who heard him, while God added his testimony by signs and wonders and various miracles, and by gifts of the Holy Spirit, distributed according to his will" (Heb 2:1-4).

Christians are invited to pay greater attention to the word they have heard. It is not enough to hear the message; it is necessary to adhere to it with all one's heart and life. Without an earnest adherence to the Gospel, there is the risk of going off course (cf. 2:1). Distancing oneself from God can lead only to losing oneself or perishing; the one who strives to adhere to the message heard comes closer to God (cf. 7:19) and finds salvation.

Having introduced his topic (cf. 2:1), the author develops it in a long sentence (cf. 2:2-4). He bases his argument on a comparison between the angels and the Lord. The only element that is identical in the two parts is the expression "declared through." The "word" was declared through angels; "salvation" began to be declared through the Lord.

When he refers to the "word," the author has in mind the promulgation of the law that occurred on Sinai. The expression "salvation" comes as a surprise. Here one would have expected a term parallel to "word." This imperfection in the parallelism is full of significance. It manifests a profound difference between the Old Testament and the New. In the old covenant, there was only a "word," an external law that commands and punishes. In the new covenant, a true salvation is offered. What excuse is there, then, for those who reject salvation? In such people, ingratitude is added to obduracy. They do not resist a requirement; they close themselves to love.

A long discourse on the topic points out three characteristics of salvation, showing how it comes to the author and to those to whom the text is directed: the Lord's preaching, the ministry of the first disciples, and the testimony on God's part (cf. 2:3b-4). The first characteristic of salvation is that it began to be declared through the Lord. The author does not use a simple verb, "to begin," but a solemn circumlocution, "to have its beginning," a subtle allusion perhaps to Genesis 1:1. Salvation constitutes a new creation. The title "Lord" designates Christ, the Son who is the final revealer sent by God (cf. Heb 1:2). The salvation revealed by him is the culmination of God's salvific work. The announcement made by the Lord reaches "us" (2:3; the author and the addressees of his text) through the ministry of the auricular witnesses, who are the first disciples of Jesus. God, from whom all revelation and salvation come (cf. 1:1-2), confirms the ministry of the disciples with signs and miracles and gifts of the Holy Spirit (cf. Acts 5:12; Rom 15:19; 1 Cor 12:4, 11; 2 Cor 12:12).

Having outlined in synthesis the whole history of revelation (Heb 1:1-2), the author shows (2:1-4) that he, and consequently his work, is linked to the Son and to God through the ministry of those witnesses who had heard the Lord.

3.7 The Book of Revelation

45. The term "inspiration" is not present in the book of Revelation, but the reality of what the term means is found there, when there is a recognition in the text of a relationship of close, direct dependence on God. We find this situation in the prologue (1:1-3); we find it again in 1:10 and 4:2, when John, in relation to what will be the content of the book, is put in special contact with the Spirit, and when, in 10:8-11, his prophetic mission is renewed in relation to the "little scroll." It recurs finally in the closing liturgical dialogue, when the intangible sacredness of the whole message is emphasized once it has reached the status of a book (22:18-19). Through contact with these passages, we come to an initial understanding of what inspiration is as presented in the book of Revelation.

3.7.1 The Divine Origin of the Text According to the Prologue (1:1-3)

A careful reading of the prologue of the book of Revelation provides us with interesting and detailed information on the path that leads, in terms of the text of Revelation, from a purely divine plane to the concrete level of a book that can be read in the liturgical assembly.

At the very beginning of the text, we can discern a first explicit contact with the level of God: the "revelation" is "of Jesus Christ" (1:1a). But Jesus Christ is not the inventor of revelation; it is God, understood as "the Father," according to constant New Testament usage. It can be said that revelation with its origin in the Father and bestowed on the Son, Jesus Christ, receives the imprint of its divine contact. From the level of God, we descend to the level of man. Here is where we meet Jesus Christ: all that is of God the Father is to be found again in him, the living "Word of God." When Jesus Christ addresses himself to human beings, he will consequently appear to them as a totally trustworthy witness, capable, insofar as he is Son at a Trinitarian level, of grasping fully the essence of the Father from whom everything derives and, as the incarnate Son, capable of communicating it adequately to humanity.

In this way Revelation enters into contact with John. And this happens in a particular way: the Father, through Jesus Christ who is its bearer, expresses revelation in symbolic "signs" which are perceived, "seen" by John, and adequately understood by him through the mediation of an angel who explains them. John, in turn, expresses the revelation of which he has come into possession in his own message to the churches, and at this point the revelation becomes a written text. The contact with the Father and the incarnate Son that gave rise to the text remains there also afterward, becoming a permanent quality of it. When the written revelation is proclaimed in the liturgical assembly in the last step of its coming into being, it will take on the form of prophecy.

3.7.2 The Transformation of John Accomplished by the Spirit Regarding Christ (1:10; 4:1-2)

46. At the beginning of the first (1:4–3:22) and second parts (4:1–22:5) of his text, the author of the book of Revelation, who identifies himself literally with John, offers an interesting clarification of the dynamic of revelation, that, starting from the Father and passing through Jesus Christ, comes at last to him: a special intervention of the Holy Spirit takes place, which, by transforming him, places John in renewed contact with Jesus Christ, with the result that he knows him better.

This is true above all at the beginning of the first part of the book (1:10), with reference to the entire section. Banished to the island of Patmos, with his mind and heart in his community of far-off

Ephesus, John, "on the Lord's day," characteristic of the liturgical assembly, becomes aware of a touch of the Spirit which happens in a new way: "I became in the spirit on the Lord's day." "To become" through the Spirit and in contact with it brings about in John an interior transformation which, even if not reaching an ecstatic level, enables him to grasp and interpret the complex symbolic sign that will be presented to him right away. From this, there will come about in John a new existential, cognitive, and affective experience of the risen Jesus Christ, from whom he will then receive the task of sending a written message to the seven churches (cf. 1:10b–3:22).

This special contact with the Spirit is renewed at the beginning (4:1-2) of the second part of the book (4:1–22:5)—"At once I became in the Spirit" (4:2)—and continues unaltered to the conclusion. The new touch of the Spirit tends, like the previous one, to transform John inwardly. It is preceded by an intervention of Jesus Christ, who tells John to transfer himself from the earth to the level of heaven. Through this second "becoming in the Spirit," John will be able to perceive the great "signs" that God will give him through Jesus Christ and express them adequately in the text. This renewing contact with the Spirit will be recalled later at certain particularly significant points in his relationship with Jesus Christ. This happens in 17:3 before the especially complex presentation of the judgment of the "great whore" (17:3–18:24), the one who, under the influence of the Demoniac, brings about the most radical opposition to the values of Jesus Christ. Then, when the great decisive "sign" of the New Jerusalem is shown, which presents the ineffable relationship of love between the Lamb Jesus Christ and the Church who has become his bride, there will be a further call to the Spirit for John (21:10), which will open him to the highest understanding of Jesus Christ. This broadening by the Spirit to perceive "something more" of Jesus Christ will pass from John to his written work and will tend to place itself in the reader-hearer.

3.7.3 Human Involvement in Enunciating the Prophetic Message (10:9-11)

47. But how does this opening in the Spirit develop in the human being? There is an interesting indication in this regard in 10:9-11.

An angel, a solemn manifestation of Christ (cf. 10:1-8), holds in his left hand a "little scroll containing a message from God, probably the still-rough content of Revelation 11:1-13, and he invites John to take it: "And he says to me: 'Take it, and eat; it will be bitter to your stomach, but sweet as honey in your mouth'" (10:9). At the first contact with the "little scroll" John is fascinated with it and experiences the inexpressible sweetness of the Word of God. But the delight of the word received will then give way to the painful toil of assimilating it. The Word of God will have to pass from the divine level to the level of human communication through an arduous elaboration from within, one requiring John's intelligence, emotive capacity, and creative literary faculties. Once this laborious phase is over, John will be able to announce the Word of God which, no longer in a crude form, has now become, through this work of elaboration, the word of man.

3.7.4 The Integrity of the Inspired Book (22:1-19)

48. Having arrived at the end of his work, when the text composed can be called "this scroll" (22:18, 19b), the author, placing everything on the lips of John, makes a radical declaration of the intangible nature of the scroll itself. Taking his initial inspiration from various texts of Deuteronomy (cf. Deut 4:2; 13:1; 29:19), the author of the book of Revelation emphasizes its radical nature: the book, by now completed, has the very completeness of God, to which one can neither add nor subtract anything. The prolonged contact that he had with Jesus Christ through the Spirit during its formation imprinted a certain sacredness on the book's message: something of Jesus Christ and of his Spirit, we may say, remains there within it, thus enabling the text to serve as a prophecy that enters into life with the capacity to change it.

3.7.5 Provenance from God: An Initial Summary

49. From what we have observed, some fundamental characteristics of the text of the book of Revelation emerge regarding the topic under consideration. The text has a marked divine origin, deriving directly from God the Father and Jesus Christ, upon whom God the

Father bestows it. Jesus Christ, in turn, bestows it on John, communicating its content in symbolic "signs," which John, with the help of the angel interpreter, succeeds in perceiving. This initial, direct contact of the text with the level of the divine becomes active throughout the course of the book, both in the first and second parts of which it is composed, by the particular and adhering influence of the Spirit, who renews and opens up John inwardly, continually producing in him a qualitative advance in his knowledge of Jesus Christ.

The content of revelation does not pass automatically from the divine level, where it comes into being and develops, to the human level, where it is heard. The development that leads to the Word of God becoming also a human word requires from John, after a burst of joy at an initial contact with the word, an arduous elaboration that brings the message to an appropriately human level and makes it comprehensible. This transition does not lead to the loss of the original characteristic: there remains in the whole text, by now definitively written and in the form of a book, a quality of sacredness which reaches the divine plane. This sacredness renders the text, on the one hand, absolutely untouchable, without the possibility of additions or subtractions, while, on the other, it activates within it the energy of prophecy that makes it fitting to leave a decisive imprint on one's life.

This complex set of characteristics, to be kept together always, allows us to see how the author of the book of Revelation senses and understands the elements of what we call today inspiration: there is an enduring intervention on the part of God the Father; there is an enduring intervention of Jesus Christ, particularly rich and well-structured; there is an intervention, also an enduring one, of the Spirit; there is an intervention of the angel interpreter; there is also, in the text's contact with humanity, a specific intervention on John's part. In the end, this text, the Word of God which has come into contact with humanity, will not only succeed in making its illuminating content known but also know how to radiate it in life. It will be inspired and inspiring.

It is striking that this last book of the New Testament, which has the greatest number of references to the Old Testament and can be seen as its synthesis, attests its provenance from God and its inspired character in a most precise and well-structured way. And a new dimension springs from this contact with Christ: the Old Testament also becomes inspired and inspiring when read in Christological terms.

IV. Conclusion

50. Concluding the section on the divine origin of the biblical books (with which we illustrate the concept of inspiration), we summarize, on the one hand, what has been shown on the relationship between God and the human authors, and we highlight in particular the fact that the writings of the New Testament recognize the inspiration of the Old Testament and read it Christologically. On the other hand, we open up a new perspective and seek to complete the results obtained up to now. A brief diachronic view of the literary formation of the biblical writings is added to the synchronic consideration. And the study of individual writings will be completed with a look at the whole collection of the writings accepted into the canon. This last aspect will be treated in two parts: the few traces of a two-testament canon that are found within the New Testament will be presented, and the history of the formation of the canon and the reception of the biblical books in Israel and in the Church will be outlined.

4.1 An Overall View of the "God–Human Author" Relationship

51. It was our intention to point out in a number of biblical books the indications of the relationship between those who wrote them and God, in order to highlight how their provenance from God is attested. From this there arose a kind of biblical phenomenology of the "God–human author" relationship. Now, after a brief summary review of what has already been discussed, we underline some characteristic traits of inspiration, coming to a conclusion about the right way with which the inspired books must be received.

4.1.1 Brief Synthesis

In the writings of the Old Testament, the relationship between the various human authors and God is expressed in several ways.

In the Pentateuch, Moses appears as the person instituted by God as the sole mediator of his revelation. In this part of the Scriptures, we find the singular assertion that God himself had written the text of the Ten Commandments and had consigned it to Moses (Exod 24:12), which attests this text's direct provenance from God. Moses is then given the task of writing other words of God (Exod 24:4; 34:27), becoming ultimately the Lord's mediator for the entire Torah (cf. Deut 31:9). The prophetic books, for their part, have a variety of formulae for expressing the fact that God communicates his word to inspired messengers who must transmit it to the people. While in the Pentateuch and in the prophetic books the Word of God is received directly by mediators chosen by God, we find a different situation in the Psalms and wisdom books. In the Psalms, the suppliant listens to the voice of God, heard above all in the great events of creation and of the saving history of Israel, but also in some particular personal experiences. Analogously, in the wisdom books, the meditative study of the Law and Prophets, inspired by the fear of God, turn the various instructions into a teaching of divine wisdom.

In the New Testament, the person of Jesus, his activity, and his journey constitute the pinnacle of divine revelation. For all the authors and writings of the New Testament, every relationship with God depends on the relationship with Jesus. The Synoptic Gospels attest their divine provenance, presenting Jesus and his revelatory work. This fact is common to all four gospels, but not without particular nuances. Matthew and Mark identify themselves with the person and work of Jesus; they present, in narrative form, his activity, his passion, and his resurrection, as the supreme divine confirmation of all his words and of all his assertions on his identity. Luke, in the prologue of his gospel, explains that his narrative is based on the encounter with eyewitnesses and ministers of the word. Finally, John claims to be an eyewitness of Jesus' work from the very beginning and, instructed by the Holy Spirit and having believed in the divine sonship of Jesus, he testifies to his revelatory work.

The other writings of the New Testament attest their provenance from Jesus and God in still different ways. Through the close connection between his two works (cf. Acts 1:1-2), Luke gives us to understand that, in the Acts of the Apostles, he is recounting the post-paschal activity of those eyewitnesses and ministers of the word (cf. Luke 1:3) on whom he depends for the presentation of Jesus' activity in his gospel. Paul attests that he received from God the Father the revelation of his Son (Gal 1:15-16) and that he had seen the risen Lord (1 Cor 9:1; 15:8), and he asserts the divine origin of his gospel. The author of the letter to the Hebrews depends on witnesses who heard the proclamation of the Lord for knowledge of the salvation revealed by God. Finally, the author of the book of Revelation describes in a subtle and varied manner how he received the revelation that is found definitively and unalterably in his book: from God the Father through Jesus Christ, in signs perceived with the help of an angel interpreter.

We find in the biblical writings, then, a wide spectrum of testimony about their divine provenance, and thus we can speak of a rich phenomenology of the relationship between God and the human author. In the Old Testament, the relationship with God is seen in various ways. In the New Testament, however, the relationship with God is always mediated by the Son of God, the Lord Jesus Christ, in whom God has spoken his final and definitive Word (cf. Heb 1:1-2). In the introduction, we mentioned the limitation of not being able to distinguish clearly between revelation and inspiration, between communication of the contents and divine assistance in the work of writing. The divine communication and the believing acceptance of the contents, which is then accompanied by the divine assistance to write it down, are fundamental. The case of the Ten Commandments, written by God himself and delivered to Moses (Exod 24:12), is wholly exceptional, and the case of the book of Revelation, in which the process is explained in detail from the divine communication to the act of writing, is also special.

4.1.2 Some Characteristic Qualities of Inspiration

52. On the basis of what has been explained succinctly above, we now indicate briefly some characteristic qualities of inspiration that can help clarify the notion of inspiration of the biblical books.

In our enquiry on the indications of the divine provenance of the various writings, we established as fundamental the living relationship with God in the Old Testament and with God through his son in the New Testament. This relationship manifests itself in various forms. For the Old Testament, we recall the form described by the Pentateuch for the unique relationship of Moses with God; the form which expresses itself in the prophetic formulae; the form of the experience of God, which is the basis of the Psalms; the form of the fear of God, which is characteristic of the wisdom books. Within this living relationship, the authors receive and recognize what they transmit in their words and in their writings. In the New Testament, the personal relationship with Jesus manifests itself in the form of discipleship, the nucleus of which is faith in Jesus Christ, the Son of God (cf. Mark 1:1; John 20:31). The relationship with Jesus can be immediate (Gospel of John; Paul) or mediated (Gospel of Luke; Letter to the Hebrews). This relationship, which is fundamental to the communication of the Word of God, appears in a particularly coherent and rich way in the Gospel of John: the author has contemplated the glory of the only-begotten Son who comes from the Father (1:14); he is an eyewitness of Jesus' journey (19:35; 21:24); he gives his testimony, instructed by the Spirit of truth (15:26-27). Here may also be seen the Trinitarian character of the relationship with God, fundamental for an inspired author of the New Testament.

According to the testimony of the biblical writings, inspiration presents itself as a special relationship with God (or with Jesus), whereby he grants to a human author to relate—through his Spirit—that which he wishes to communicate to human beings. In this way, what *Dei Verbum* asserts (n. 11) is confirmed: the books are written through the inspiration of the Holy Spirit; God is their author, because he employs chosen people, acting in and through them; these, however, write as true authors.

The characteristics we have observed in our study appear complementary: (a) the gift of a personal relationship with God (unconditional faith in God, fear of God, faith in Jesus Christ Son of God) is fundamental; (b) in this relationship, the author embraces the various ways in which God reveals himself (creation, history, presence of Jesus of Nazareth); and (c) in the plan of God's revelation, which culminates in the sending of his Son Jesus, both the personal relationship with God and the manner of revelation undergo some variations, according to the phases and circumstances of revelation. From this, one concludes that inspiration is analogously the same for all the authors of the biblical books (as indicated in *Dei Verbum*, n. 11) but with various facets owing to the plan of divine revelation.

4.1.3 The Right Way to Receive the Inspired Books

53. In our study of the inspiration of the biblical writings, we have seen God's tireless concern to address himself to his people, and we have also considered the Spirit in which these books were written.

God's solicitude should be received with a deep gratitude, manifested in a keen interest and great attention, to hear and to understand what God wants to communicate to us. The Spirit in which the books were written, however, should be the Spirit in which we listen to them. True disciples of Jesus, profoundly moved by faith in their Lord, wrote the books of the New Testament. These books are meant to be heard by true disciples of Jesus (cf. Matt 28:19), filled with living faith in him (cf. John 20:31). It is with the risen Jesus, according to the teaching that Jesus gave his disciples (cf. Luke 24:25-27, 44-47) and from his perspective, that we are called to read the writings of the Old Testament. For the scientific study of the biblical writings too, conducted not in a neutral way but with a truly theological approach, it is essential to take account of inspiration. Indeed, the criterion of an authentic reading is indicated by *Dei Verbum* when it affirms that "Holy Scripture must be read and interpreted in the same Spirit in which it was written" (n. 12). Modern exegetical methods cannot take the place of faith, but, when applied within the framework of faith, they can be very fruitful for the theological understanding of the texts.

4.2 The Writings of the New Testament Attest the Inspiration of the Old Testament and Interpret It Christologically

54. In the study of the New Testament writings, we have always found that they refer to the Sacred Scriptures of the Jewish tradition. Here, in conclusion, we offer some examples in which the

relationship to texts of the Old Testament is made explicit. We will conclude commenting on two passages of the New Testament that not only cite the Old Testament, but clearly affirm its inspiration.

4.2.1 Some Examples

Matthew cites the prophets in a typical way. In fact, when he speaks of the fulfillment of the promises or the prophecies, he does not attribute them to a prophet (writing: "As the prophet says/said") but, explicitly or implicitly, ascribes them to God himself by using the theological passive: "All this took place to fulfill what had been spoken by the Lord *through the prophet*" (Matt 1:22; 2:15; 2:17; 8:17; 12:17; 13:35; 21:4); the prophet is only the instrument of God. By presenting what came about with Jesus as the fulfillment of the ancient promise, he gives it a Christological interpretation.

The Gospel of Luke adds that this interpretation originates with Jesus himself, who describes his ministry using the oracles of Isaiah (Luke 4:18-19) or the prophetic figures of Elijah and Elisha (Luke 4:25-27); with all the authority his resurrection gives him, he shows finally how all the Scriptures speak of him, his sufferings and his glory (Luke 24:25-27, 44-47).

In John, Jesus himself affirms that the Scriptures bear witness to him; he does this arguing with his interlocutors, who scrutinize these Scriptures to obtain eternal life (John 5:39).

Paul, as has already been abundantly demonstrated, unhesitatingly recognizes the authority of the Scriptures, attests their divine origin, and sees them as prophecies of the Gospel.

4.2.2 The Testimony of 2 Timothy 3:15-16 and 2 Peter 1:20-21

55. In these two letters (2 Tim and 2 Pet), we find the only explicit attestations of the inspired nature of the Old Testament Scriptures. Paul reminds Timothy of his formation in the faith, saying: "From childhood you have known the sacred writings that are able to instruct you for salvation through faith in Christ Jesus. All scripture is inspired by God and is useful for teaching, for reproof, for correction, and for training in righteousness" (2 Tim 3:15-16). The Sacred Scriptures of

the Old Testament, read with faith in Christ Jesus, formed the basis of Timothy's religious teaching (cf. Acts 16:1-3; 2 Tim 1:5) and served to strengthen his faith in Christ. By characterizing all these Scriptures as "inspired," Paul is saying that the Spirit of God is their author. Peter bases his apostolic message (which proclaims "the power and coming of our Lord Jesus Christ"; 2 Pet 1:16) on his own eye-witness and auricular testimony and on the word of the prophets. He mentions (1:16-18) his own presence on the holy mountain of the Transfiguration, when, along with other witnesses ("we"; 1:18), he heard the voice of God the Father: "This is my Son, my Be-loved" (1:17). Reference is then made to the very secure word of the prophets (1:19), of which he says, "First of all you must understand this, that no prophecy of scripture is a matter of one's own interpre-tation, because no prophecy ever came by human will, but men and women moved by the Holy Spirit spoke from God" (1:20-21). He speaks of all the prophecies that are found in Scripture and attributes them to the influence of the Holy Spirit in the prophets. It is the same God whose voice Peter heard on the mountain of the Transfiguration who spoke through the prophets. From this same God, through these two mediations, the apostolic message about Christ comes.

The fact—common to 2 Timothy and 2 Peter—that the authors speak of the "Scriptures," while drawing attention to their own ap-ostolic work, is important for the relationship between the Old Tes-tament and the apostolic testimony. Paul first mentions his teaching and exemplary life (2 Tim 3:10-11) and then the role of the Scriptures (3:16-17). Peter presents himself as an eyewitness of the Transfigura-tion (2 Pet 1:16-18) and then makes reference to the ancient prophets (1:19-21). Both texts show that, for Christians, the immediate context for the reading and interpretation of the inspired Scriptures (of the Old Testament) is the apostolic testimony. From this one deduces that also this latter should be understood as inspired.

4.3 The Process of the Literary Formation of the
Biblical Writings and Inspiration

56. A brief diachronic survey of the literary formation of the biblical writings shows that the canon of Scripture was established

gradually, stage by stage, over the course of history. Regarding the Old Testament, these steps may be schematically presented as follows:

- the writing down of oral traditions, of prophetic words, of law collections
- the establishment of collections of written traditions, which gradually acquire authority and are recognized as expressions of divine revelation; this applies to the Torah
- a connection between the various collections: Torah, Prophets, and Wisdom writings

The oldest traditions, however, have been the object of continual rereadings and multiple reinterpretations. The same phenomenon occurs even within certain literary collections: thus, in the Torah, the more recent law collections present a development and interpretation of the pre-exilic laws; or again, in the book of Isaiah we find traces of successive developments and of a literary work of unification.

Finally, the latest writings present an actualization of the ancient texts; the book of Sirach, for example, identifies the Torah with Wisdom.

The study of the New Testament traditions has shown how these are based on the written traditions of Judaism in order to announce the Gospel of Christ. We can recall, in this regard, that the Luke-Acts diptych refers frequently to the Torah, the prophetic literature, and the Psalms to show how Jesus "fulfilled" the Scriptures of Israel (Luke 24:25-27, 44).

To understand the notion of the inspiration of the Sacred Scriptures, then, we must take into consideration this movement within the Scriptures themselves. Inspiration concerns each particular text, as well as the whole canon, which links Old Testament and New Testament traditions together. The ancient traditions of Israel, handed on in writing, have in fact been reread, commented on, and finally interpreted in the light of the mystery of Christ, who gives them their *full*, definitive meaning.

It is by following certain "trails" or "lines" within Scripture that the reader can bring out the way in which the theological themes are broadened and developed. The canonical reading of the Bible allows us to highlight the progress of revelation by means of a logic, both diachronic and synchronic.

We give a single example. The theology of creation, announced from the beginning of the book of Genesis, is developed in the prophetic literature; chapter 43 of the book of Isaiah, in fact, connects salvation and creation, understanding the salvation of Israel as a prolongation of creation, while chapters 65–66 interpret the hoped-for rebirth of Israel as a new creation (Isa 65:17; 66:22). This theology is then further developed in the Psalms and wisdom literature.

57. In the New Testament, one can point out, on the one hand, a "relationship of fulfillment" with the Old Testament traditions and, on the other hand, a diachronic movement of development and reinterpretation of the traditions analogous to that specified for the Old Testament.

To illustrate the relationship of fulfillment between the New Testament writings and traditions of the Old Testament, we can cite the Gospel of John, which, in its prologue, presents Christ as the creative Word, and also the Pauline letters, which call to mind the cosmic significance of Christ's coming (cf. 1 Cor 8:6; Col 1:12-20), and even the book of Revelation, which describes the victory of Christ as the eschatological renewal of creation (Rev 21).

The diachronic study of the books of the New Testament shows that they assimilated ancient, sometimes preliterary, traditions, which reflect the life and the liturgical expressions of the primitive Christian community: the First Letter to the Corinthians, for example, cites an ancient profession of faith in 15:3-5. On the other hand, the books included in the canon of the New Testament reflect a progression and an evolution in the theological and institutional development of the first communities; thus, the letters to Timothy or to Titus attest ministerial functions and procedures of discernment that are more developed than those in the first letters written by Paul.

This brief diachronic survey must be linked to a perspective of synchronic reading: insofar as the canon of Scripture is framed between the book of Genesis and the book of Revelation, the reader of the Bible is encouraged to understand it as a whole, as a single account that unfolds from creation up to the new creation inaugurated by Christ.

The inspiration of Sacred Scripture refers, therefore, to each of the texts that constitute it, as well as to the canon as a whole. To affirm that a biblical book is inspired means to recognize that it constitutes a specific and privileged vehicle of God's revelation to humankind and that its human authors were impelled by the Spirit to express truths of faith in a historically located text and received as normative by believing communities.

To assert that Scripture, as a whole, is inspired, is equivalent to recognizing that it constitutes a canon, that is, a collection of writings that are normative for the faith and received in the Church. The Bible as such is the place of the revelation of an unsurpassable truth, identified in a person—Jesus Christ—who, by his words and deeds, "fulfills" and "perfects" the traditions of the Old Testament by revealing the Father fully.

4.4 Toward a Two-Testament Canon

58. The two letters 2 Timothy and 2 Peter play important roles in the first outline of a Christian canon of Scripture. They hint at the closure of a body of Pauline and Petrine letters, impede any later addition to these letters, and prepare for the closure of the canon. The text of 2 Peter in particular points toward a two-testament canon and an ecclesial reception of the Pauline letters, an important factor in the reception of these writings in the Church. The majority of biblical exegetes consider the two letters as "pseudepigraphical" works (attributed to the apostles but actually produced by later authors). This does not jeopardize their inspired character and does not diminish their theological significance.

4.4.1 The Closure of the Collections of the Pauline and Petrine Letters

Both letters look back to the past and highlight the imminent end of the lives of the two authors. They make frequent use of "remembering" and exhort the readers to remember and apply the teaching that the apostles communicated to them in the past (cf. 2 Tim 1:6, 13; 2:2, 8, 14; 3:14; 2 Pet 1:12, 15; 3:1-2). Insofar as the two letters insistently signal the death of the authors, they serve effectively as a conclusion for the collection of the respective letters.

In 2 Timothy, Paul's death is presented as imminent: the apostle, abandoned by his helpers and having lost his case at the imperial court (cf. 4:16-18), is ready to receive the crown of martyrdom: "As for me, I am already being poured out like a libation, and the time of my departure has come. I have fought the good fight, I have finished the race, I have kept the faith. From now on there is reserved for me the crown of righteousness, which the Lord, the righteous judge, will give me on that day" (4:6-8). Similarly, 2 Peter indicates that the Lord has revealed the proximity of the apostle's death: "I think it right, as long as I am in this body, to refresh your memory, since I know that my death will come soon, as indeed our Lord Jesus Christ has made clear to me. And I will make every effort so that after my departure you may be able at any time to recall these things" (1:13-15; cf. 3:1).

Both of these letters thus appear to be the last letters of their respective authors, their testaments, which bring to a close what they intended to communicate.

4.4.2 Toward a Two-Testament Canon

59. In 2 Peter 3:2, Peter indicates the purpose of his two letters: "that you should remember the words spoken in the past by the holy prophets, and the commandment of the Lord and Savior spoken through your apostles." Although the text speaks of words spoken by the prophets, there is no doubt that the author is thinking of the prophetic Scriptures (cf. 1:20). The term "commandment of the Lord and Savior" does not designate a specific commandment of the Lord but has the same meaning as in the preceding passage, in which "the knowledge of our Lord and Savior Jesus Christ" is indicated as "the way of righteousness" and "the holy commandment that was passed on to them" (2:20-21). The term "commandment" (in the singular), coined in analogy to Torah, has an almost technical significance, and in 3:2, linked to a double genitive, it indicates the teaching of Christ transmitted by the apostles, that is, the Gospel as the new plan of salvation.

Second Peter 3:2 highlights the prophets, the Lord, the apostles. In this way the canon of the two Testaments is delineated: the first is determined by the prophets and the second by the Lord and Savior Jesus, attested by the apostles. Both Testaments are intimately connected through their witness to faith in Christ (cf. 2 Pet 1:16-21; 3:1-2), the Old Testament (the prophets) through a Christological reading, and the New Testament through the testimony of the apostles, expressed in their letters (especially those of Peter and Paul), but also in the gospels, based on "eyewitnesses and ministers of the word" (Luke 1:2; cf. John 1:14).

Second Peter 3:15-16 is also important for the conception of the two-testament canon and its inspired character. Peter, having explained the delay of the *parousia* (3:3-14), affirms his agreement with Paul: "So also our beloved brother Paul wrote to you according to the wisdom given him, speaking of this as he does in all his letters. There are some things in them hard to understand, which the ignorant and unstable twist to their own destruction, as they do the other scriptures." Affirmed here is the existence of a collection of Pauline letters which the people whom Peter addresses have received. The assertion that Paul wrote "according to the wisdom given to him" presents him as an inspired writer. The false interpretations of difficult Pauline passages are equated with those "of the other scriptures"; in this way, the Pauline texts and the letter of Peter, confirmed by them, are placed alongside the "scriptures" which, like prophetic texts, are inspired by God (cf. 1:20-21).

4.5 The Reception of the Biblical Books and the Formation of the Canon

60. The books which today make up our Sacred Scriptures do not authenticate themselves as "canonical." Their authority, on account of their inspiration, must be recognized and accepted by the community, whether it be the synagogue or the Church. It is right, then, to consider the historical process of this recognition.

Every literature has its classic books. A classic comes from the cultural world of a specific people, but at the same time it broadens the language of that society and imposes itself as a model for future writers. A book becomes a classic not by decree of some authority but because it is recognized as such by the more cultivated members of the people. Many religions too have, so to speak, their classics. In this case, the writings chosen are those that reflect the beliefs of the adherents of those religions, who find there the sources of their religious practices. This happened in the ancient Near East, in Mesopotamia, and even in Egypt. The same phenomenon occurred for the Jews, who, with a special awareness of being the chosen people of God, identified themselves substantially with their religious tradition. From among the various writings conserved in their archives, the scribes selected those that contained sacred laws, the narrative of their national history, the prophetic oracles, and the collection of wisdom sayings in which the Jewish people could mirror themselves and recognize the origins of their faith. The same happened among Christians of the first centuries, with the apostolic writings now contained in the New Testament.

4.5.1 The Pre-Exilic Period

Scholars consider it possible that such a selection of written and oral traditions, among them the prophetic sayings and many Psalms, had already begun before the Exile. Indeed Jeremiah 18:18 says: "For instruction shall not perish from the priest, nor counsel from the wise, nor the word from the prophet." The reform of Josiah had as its basis the book of the Covenant (Deuteronomy perhaps), rediscovered in the temple (2 Kgs 23:2).

4.5.2 The Post-Exilic Period

It is on the return from the Exile, under Persian domination, that we can speak of the beginnings of the formation of a tripartite canon consisting of Law, Prophets, and Writings (mainly of a wisdom nature). Those who had returned from Babylon needed to rediscover their identity as the people of the Covenant. It was necessary, therefore, to codify laws, requested also by the Persian overlords. The collection of historical records reconnected them with pre-exilic Judah; the prophetic books served to explain the reasons for the deportation, while the Psalms were indispensable for worship in the reconstructed temple. And because it was believed that from the reign of Artaxerxes (465–423 BC) prophecy had ceased and the spirit had passed to the sages (cf. Josephus Flavius, *Contr. Ap.* 1.8.41; *Ant.* 13:311-13), various wisdom books began to be produced by erudite scribes. These people took upon themselves the task of collecting those books which, on account of their antiquity, religious veneration, and authority, could provide a precise identity for the returning exiles, as well as for their new overlords. Political and social motives, therefore, are not to be excluded from the initial formation of the canon. We can then consider the governorship of Nehemiah as the *terminus a quo* for the formation of the canon. In fact, 2 Maccabees 2:13-15 tells us that Nehemiah founded a library, gathering together all the books about the kings and the prophets and the writings of David, as well as the letters of kings about votive offerings. Moreover, as at the time of Josiah, the scribe Ezra read the book of the law of Moses to the people with authority (Neh 8).

The post-exilic scribes did not limit themselves to collecting the books endowed with religious authority. They updated the laws and historical narratives, assembled prophetic oracles, and added passages of interpretive comment and with various materials composed a single book (for example, the book of Isaiah and the Twelve Prophets). Moreover, they composed new psalms and gave shape to wisdom books. They unified everything under the names of Moses, lawgiver and greatest prophet; David, the psalmist; and Solomon, the wise ruler. Such a complex literary *corpus* turned out very useful for supporting the faith also in the face of the cultural challenges of the Persian and Hellenistic eras. At the same time they began to establish the text of the more ancient books, and thus the canon and the text developed together.

4.5.3 The Maccabean Period

A new problem arose when Antiochus IV had all the sacred books of the Jews destroyed. A reorganization became necessary, therefore, and this brings us to the *terminus ad quem* of the Old Testament era. Already in the first decades of the second century BC,

Sirach classified the sacred books as Law, Prophets, and other later writings (prologue). In Sirach 44–50, he recapitulates the history of Israel from the beginning down to his own times, and in 48:1-11, he explicitly mentions the prophet Elijah; in 48:20-25, Isaiah; and in 49:7-10, Jeremiah, Ezekiel, and the Twelve Prophets. About fifty years later, 1 Maccabees 1:56-57 tells us that during the persecution of Antiochus, the Seleucids burned the books of the law and the book of the Covenant, but 2 Maccabees 2:14 tells us that Judas Maccabeus collected the books saved from the persecution.

In the first century of the Christian era, Josephus Flavius mentions that there are twenty-two books acknowledged as sacred by the Jews (*Contr. Ap.* 1.37–43), books containing laws, narrative traditions, hymns, and counsels. That number is explained by the fact that many books which in our editions of the Bible are separate (e.g., the Twelve Prophets) count as a single book. The number 22 can indicate completeness, because it corresponds to the letters of the Hebrew alphabet. Today, the tendency is to date the closure of the rabbinic canon to the second century AD, or even later, either for reasons internal to Judaism, or as a reaction to the Christian acceptance of the books of the New Testament as Sacred Scripture. The distinction that used to be made between a Palestinian canon of twenty-two books and a larger one in the Diaspora no longer finds favor today, especially after the discovery of Qumran.

4.5.4 The Old Testament Canon in the Fathers

Among the Fathers of the Church too we find some divergence between those who accepted a shorter canon, perhaps to be able to engage in dialogue with the Jews, and those who included also the deuterocanonical books (written in Greek) among those received by the Church. At the Council of Hippo in 393, at which Augustine, then a simple priest, was present, the bishops of Africa, by establishing the criterion of the public reading in the majority of churches or in the principal churches, provided the basis for the reception of the deuterocanonical books, which was definitively affirmed in the medieval era. In the Catholic Church it was the Council of Trent that decided to approve the longer canon against the reformers who had returned to the shorter one. The majority of Orthodox Churches do not differ from the Catholic Church, but some divergence exists among the ancient Eastern Churches.

4.5.5 The Formation of the New Testament Canon

61. Moving on to the formation of the books of the New Testament, we note the fact that the content of these books was received before it was put down in writing, since those who believed accepted the preaching of Christ and the apostles before the composition of our sacred books. One need only think of the prologue of Luke, where he affirms that his gospel does not intend to do anything other than to provide through its account of the story of Jesus a "solid foundation" for the teachings which Theophilus has received. Although many may have been occasional writings, they expressed an inner need of the Christian communities to add a *didaché* (written teaching) to the *kerygma* (proclamation). Read initially for the assemblies to which they were directed, these writings were gradually transmitted to other churches because of their apostolic authority. The acceptance of these documents—because they spoke with the authority of Jesus and of the apostles—should not, however, be identified with their reception as "Scripture" on a par with the Old Testament. We have mentioned the intimations in 2 Peter 3:2, 15-16, but we must wait until the end of the second century for this conviction of their equality to be generalized and for the books comprising the "Old Testament" and those making up the "New Testament" to be put on the same level.

During the first century after Christ, the "volumen" (which had the form of a scroll) gave way to the "codex" (consisting of bound pages, as is usual for books today); this contributed a great deal to the production of small literary collections that could be contained in a single book, first and foremost the gospels and the letters of Paul. Indications of the constitution of a *corpus johanneum* and of the "Catholic epistles" come later.

The need to define the limits of the collection of authoritative writings arose when, at the beginning of the second century, the Gnostics, to spread their doctrines, began to compose works in the same literary genres as the great Church (gospels, acts, letters, and apocalypses). At this time the need for definite criteria to distinguish the orthodox texts from the heterodox was felt. Some extreme Jewish-Christian groups, such as the Ebionites, wanted the *damnatio memoriae* of Paul, while the Montanists attributed excessive importance to charismatic gifts. The author who had a decisive influence in keeping alive the doctrine of Paul was Luke, with his Acts of the Apostles, which in large part describes the activity of this apostle and the success of his mission. Marcion also contributed in his own way to the process of the reception of New Testament texts with his choice of Paul and Luke as the only "canonical" books, because he brought about a reaction that served to clarify which writings were already venerated by Christians. Criteria for this discernment were gradually established, among which were public and universal reading, apostolicity understood as the authentic tradition of an apostle, and especially the *regula fidei* (Irenaeus), that is, that the text does not contradict the apostolic tradition transmitted by the bishops in all the churches. With respect to this *catholicitas* Marcion's position was inadequate, since he limited the apostolic tradition to the Pauline tradition alone and overlooked the Petrine, Johannine, and Jewish-Christian traditions.

From the end of the second century onward, lists of New Testament books begin to appear. The four gospels, Acts, and thirteen Pauline epistles were universally accepted, while there was some hesitation regarding Hebrews, the Catholic Epistles, and also the book of Revelation. In some lists, the first letter of Clement, the Shepherd of Hermas, and some other writings were also added. These texts, however, were not taken up into the canon, since they were not read universally. On the basis of a general consensus of the churches, expressed in numerous declarations of the Magisterium and attested in important pronouncements of various local synods, the Council of Hippo (at the end of the fourth century) fixed the Canon of the New Testament, which was then confirmed by the dogmatic definition of the Council of Trent.

Unlike the Old Testament canon, the twenty-seven books of the New Testament are held to be canonical by Catholics, Orthodox, and Protestants. The reception of these books on the part of the believing community expresses the recognition of their divine inspiration and their character as sacred and normative books.

For the Catholic Church, as stated already, the definitive, official recognition of both the "long" canon of the Old Testament and the twenty-seven writings of the New Testament occurred in the Council of Trent (*D-S* 1501–3). The definition had been made necessary by the reformers' exclusion of the deuterocanonical books from the traditional canon.

Part Two

The Testimony of the Biblical Writings to Their Truth

62. In this second part of our document, we intend to illustrate how the biblical writings attest the truth of their message. After the introduction, we will show in the first section how some books of the Old Testament present the truth revealed by God in preparation for the Gospel revelation (cf. *DV*, n. 3), and in the second section, we will illustrate what several New Testament writings say about the truth revealed through Jesus Christ, who brings divine revelation to fulfillment (cf. *DV*, n. 4).

I. Introduction

To introduce our topic, we examine first of all what *Dei Verbum* understands by biblical truth, and then we specify the thematic focus that will be given to our examination of the biblical writings.

1.1 Biblical Truth According to Dei Verbum

63. The truth of the Word of God in the Sacred Scriptures is intimately linked to their inspiration: the God who speaks cannot, in fact, deceive. Notwithstanding this broad declaration, various pronouncements of the sacred text create difficulties. The Fathers of the Church were already aware of these, and the problems persist today, as shown by the discussions that took place during the Second

Vatican Council. What follows will seek to clarify the meaning of the term "truth" as understood by the Council.

Theologians have had recourse to the concept of "inerrancy," applying it to Sacred Scripture. If it is taken in its absolute sense, this term would suggest that there can be no error of any kind in the Bible. But with the progressive discoveries in the field of history, philology, and the natural sciences, and because of the application to biblical research of the historical-critical method, exegetes have had to recognize that not everything in the Bible is expressed in accordance with the demands of the contemporary sciences, because the biblical writers reflect the limits of their own personal knowledge, in addition to those of their time and culture. The Second Vatican Council had to confront this problem in the preparation of the dogmatic constitution *Dei Verbum.*

Paragraph 11 of *Dei Verbum* proposes the traditional doctrine that the Church, "relying on the belief of the apostles, holds that the books of both the Old and New Testaments in their entirety, with all their parts, are sacred and canonical because, having been written under the inspiration of the Holy Spirit (cf. John 20:31; 2 Tim 3:16; 2 Pet 1:19-20, 3:15-16), they have God as their author." The Constitution does not enter into the details of the manner of inspiration (cf. the encyclical of Pope Leo XIII *Providentissimus Deus*), but in the same paragraph 11 it says: "Therefore, since everything asserted by the inspired authors or sacred writers must be held to be asserted by the Holy Spirit, it follows that the books of Scripture must be acknowledged as teaching firmly, faithfully, and without error that truth which God wanted put into the sacred writings for the sake of our salvation. Therefore 'all Scripture is inspired by God and useful for teaching, for reproving, for correcting, for instruction in justice; so that [everyone who belongs to] God may be perfect, equipped for every good work' (2 Tim 3:16-17, Greek text)."

The Theological Commission had eliminated the expression "saving truth" (*veritas salutaris*), introducing a longer formulation: "the truth which God wanted put into the sacred writings for the sake of our salvation" (*veritatem quam Deus nostrae salutis causa Litteris Sacris consignari voluit*). Since the same Commission explained that the parenthetical clause "for the sake of our salvation" refers to "truth," this means that when one speaks of the "truth of the Sacred Scripture," one has in mind the truth that concerns our salvation. This must not, however, be taken to mean that the truth of Sacred Scripture concerns only those parts of the Sacred Book that are necessary for faith and morality, to the exclusion of other parts (the expression *veritas salutaris* of the fourth schema had not been accepted precisely to avoid such an interpretation). The meaning of the expression "the truth which God wanted put into sacred writings for the sake of our salvation" is rather that the books of Scripture, with all their parts, insofar as they are inspired by the Holy Spirit and have God as their author, intend to communicate the truth insofar as it relates to our salvation, which is, in fact, the purpose for which God reveals himself.

To confirm this thesis, *Dei Verbum* 11 cites in note 21 not just 2 Timothy 3:16-17 but *De Genesi ad litteram* 2.9.20 and *Epistula* 82.3 of St. Augustine, which excludes from biblical teaching all that is not useful for our salvation; and St. Thomas, basing himself on the first citation of St. Augustine, says in *De veritate* q. 12, a. 2, *Illa vero, quae ad salutem pertinere non possunt, sunt extranea a materia prophetiae* ("Those things, however, that cannot pertain to salvation are alien to the matter of prophecy").

64. The problem, then, is to understand what "truth for the sake of our salvation" means in the context of *Dei Verbum*. It is not enough to consider the term "truth" in its common sense: since we are dealing with Christian truth, the concept is enriched by the biblical meaning of truth and even more by the use which the Council makes of it in other documents. In the Old Testament, God himself is the highest truth because of the steadfastness of his choices, promises, and gifts; his words are truthful, and they require, in the response of human beings, a reciprocal steadfast acceptance in one's heart and in one's actions (see, e.g., 2 Sam 7:28; Ps 31:6). Truth is the foundation of the Covenant. In the New Testament, Christ himself is the truth, because he is the Amen incarnate of all God's promises (see 2 Cor 1:19-20) and because he, who is "the way, the truth, and the life" (John 14:6), by revealing the Father (John 1:18) gives access to him (John 14:6) who is the ultimate source of life (John 5:26; 6:57). The Spirit that Christ gives is the Spirit of truth

(John 14:17; 15:26; 16:13), who will endorse the testimony of the apostles (John 15:26-27) and the steadfastness of our own faith response. The truth, then, has a Trinitarian yet essentially Christological dimension, and the Church that proclaims it is "the pillar and bulwark of the truth" (1 Tim 3:15). Christ, foretold in the Old Testament, is therefore the revealer and the object of the truth for our salvation: the truth is manifested in the New Testament in his person and in the Kingdom, present and eschatological, announced and inaugurated by him. The Second Vatican Council's concept of truth is understood within the same Trinitarian, Christological, and ecclesial setting (see *Dei Verbum*, nn. 2, 7, 8, 19, 24; *Gaudium et Spes*, n. 3; *Dignitatis Humanae*, n. 11): the Son in person reveals the Father, and his revelation is communicated and confirmed by the Holy Spirit and handed on in the Church.

1.2 The Focus of Our Study of Biblical Truth

65. Our detailed study of the topic, carried out through several biblical writings, is based on the teaching and thrust of *Dei Verbum* just outlined. First of all, we cite the phrase with which the aforesaid Constitution concludes the first passage on revelation: "By this revelation then, the deepest truth about God and the salvation of man is made clear to us in Christ, who is the Mediator and at the same time the fullness of all revelation (cf. Matt 11:27; John 1:14, 17; 14:6; 17:1-3; 2 Cor 3:16; 4:6; Eph 1:3-14)" (n. 2). There is no doubt that the truth which is at the center of revelation and, consequently, at the center of the Bible, as an instrument for the transmission of revelation (cf. *DV*, nn. 7–10), concerns God and the salvation of humankind. And there is no doubt that the fullness of this truth manifests itself through and in Christ. He is the Word of God in person (John 1:1, 14) who comes from God and reveals God. He not only speaks the truth about God, but is the truth about God, he who asserts "Whoever has seen me has seen the Father" (John 14:9; cf. 12:45). The coming of the Son also reveals the salvation of humanity: "God so loved the world that he gave his only Son, so that everyone who believes in him may not perish but may have eternal life" (John 3:16).

In our study of the truth of the biblical writings, our attention will now be focused on these two themes which are intimately connected to one another: what the writings say about God and what they say about God's plan for the salvation of humanity. The fullness of revelation and of truth was brought by Christ; but his coming was prepared by a prolonged divine revelation attested by the writings of the Old Testament. Therefore, we also wish to hear what these writings have to say about God and about salvation, aware that the full significance of what they attest is revealed in the person and work of Christ. Not only the final goal, but also the way and the preparation form an essential part of God's revelation.

II. The Testimony of Select Old Testament Texts

66. From the immense riches of the Bible, we have chosen a few representative books, keeping in mind the different literary genres and the importance of the texts. A number of central themes concerning God and salvation will be explored, as they are spoken of in the accounts of creation (Gen 1–2), the Decalogues, the historical and prophetic books, the Psalms, the Song of Songs, and the wisdom writings. Although the Old Testament is the preparation for the culminating event of God's revelation in Christ, the consideration of its greater breadth and of the variety and richness of its texts has led us to consider a larger number of Old Testament than New Testament passages. Our intention is to show that the different texts reveal God and his salvation and contribute to a growth of awareness and understanding of this subject.

2.1 The Creation Accounts (Gen 1–2)

67. The first pages of the Bible, which contain the so-called creation accounts (Gen 1–2), attest faith in the God who is the origin and goal of all. As "creation accounts," they do not show "how" the world and humanity began but speak of the Creator and his relationship with what he had created. Much misunderstanding results from reading these texts from a modern perspective, seeing them as affirmations of "how" the world and humanity were formed.

To respond more adequately to the intention of the biblical texts, it is necessary to oppose such a reading, but without putting their assertions in competition with the knowledge that has come from the natural sciences of our time. These do not suppress the Bible's claim to communicate the truth, because the truth of the biblical accounts of creation concerns the meaningful coherence of the world as a work created by God.

The first creation account (Gen 1:1–2:4a), through its well-organized structure, describes not *how* the world came into being but *why* and *for what purpose* it is as it is. In poetic style, using the imagery of his era, the author of Genesis 1:1–2:4a shows that God is the origin of the cosmos and of humankind. God the Creator, of whom the Bible speaks, is oriented toward having a relationship with his creatures, in such a way that his act of creation, as the Bible describes it, emphasizes this relationship. By creating humanity "in his image" and entrusting humans with the task of taking care of creation, God manifests his fundamental saving will.

The principal elements of human existence are at the center of the account of Genesis 1, which reaches its climax with the anthropological affirmation that humankind is the "image of God," that is, his deputy in creation. According to the account, the first work of God the Creator is time (Gen 1:3-5), as indicated by the alternation of light and darkness. But this does not really describe what time is. The distribution of the various works of creation over six days does not intend to affirm as a truth to be believed that the world really took form in six days, while God rested on the seventh; it intends to communicate, rather, that there exists an order and a purpose in creation. Humans can and must participate in this order, to acknowledge, in the transition from work to rest, that the time that God has structured for them allows them to understand themselves as creatures who owe their existence to the Creator.

Each one of the works of creation portrays its nature and its purpose. The whole narrative, as has already been said, is oriented toward humanity. Thus the creation account seeks not to give a physical definition of the category of space but to present it as "living space" for humanity and to point out its meaning. The so-called charge of dominating the earth (Gen 1:28) is a metaphor expressing humanity's responsibility toward the living space assigned to humans, as well as to animals and plants.

The two creation accounts (Gen 1:1–2:4a; Gen 2:4b-25) introduce the canonical collection of the Hebrew Bible and, more broadly, that of the Christian Bible. Using various images, they seek to declare the same truth: the created world is a gift of God, and the divine plan has the good of humanity as its goal (Gen 2:18), as is clear, among other things, from the frequent recourse to the adjective "good" (Gen 1:4-21). Humanity is thus placed in a "relationship of creation" with God: the original and free gift of the Creator calls for humanity's response.

2.2 The Decalogues (Exod 20:2-17; Deut 5:6-21)

68. The two Decalogues of Exodus 20:2-17 and Deuteronomy 5:6-21 introduce the different legislative collections, brought together partly in the books of Exodus, Leviticus, and Numbers (Exod 19:1–Num 10:10) and partly in the book of Deuteronomy (Deut 12–26). These texts take the form of a discourse of the Lord (YHWH), who sometimes addresses Israel in the first person and sometimes through Moses the intermediary. This literary form confers on such texts a very strong *status of authority*. The Decalogues constitute a point of connection between a summary of Israel's faith (Exod 20:2 = Deut 5:6) which makes reference to the stories of the Exodus, on the one hand, and the collection of cultic and ethical prescriptions on the other. These Decalogues have numerous points in common, and, at the same time, each has its own specific theology: in fact, while the Decalogue of Exodus 20 develops mainly a *theology of creation*, the Decalogue of Deuteronomy 5 insists mostly on the *theology of salvation*.

The two Decalogues, being well-developed theological syntheses, are considered "summaries" of the Torah and provide theological keys that permit their correct interpretation.

2.2.1 The Literary Construction of the Two Decalogues

The introduction of the Decalogues (Exod 20:2 = Deut 5:6) defines the Lord (YHWH) as the saving God of history: the God of Israel makes himself known through the work of salvation that he accomplishes for the benefit of Israel. This narrative presentation of the God of Israel as Savior of his people summarizes the whole first part of the book of Exodus: the formula of the Lord's self-presentation in Exodus 3:14, "I AM WHO I AM," introduces the long account of the liberation of Israel (Exod 4–14). The Lord reveals his true identity, bestowing on his people the gift of salvation. The *gift of God* constitutes, therefore, the foundation of the legislative prescriptions received in the Decalogues. This gift of God consists in the liberation granted to Israel, reduced to slavery in Egypt. The laws of the Decalogue, in their turn, set out the manner of Israel's response to the gift of God: Israel, freed by God, must now enter upon this path of freedom, renouncing idols and evil (see, on this point, Pontifical Biblical Commission, *The Bible and Morality: Biblical Roots of Christian Conduct*, n. 20).

The first section of the text develops the prohibitions against idolatry, the making of images, and solicits a strict monotheism (Exod 20:3-7 = Deut 5:7-11). To renounce idols means to consent to the exclusive worship of the Lord and to accept a definitive covenant with him; the Lord is the only Savior of the people, the *only true God*.

The two positive commandments of the Decalogue concern the Sabbath and respect toward parents (Exod 20:8-12 and Deut 5:12-16). The Sabbath day can be defined as the "sanctuary of God" in time and in history; by respecting the Sabbath, Israel shows that only the Lord can give meaning to human history.

The last section of the text of the Decalogues concerns the mode of the right relationship with one's neighbor (Exod 20:13-17; Deut 5:17-21). The renunciation of every oppressive design against one's neighbor is the indispensable condition for the construction of a true community, in testimony of the possible victory of fraternal love over violence.

2.2.2 Commentary and Theological Implications

69. The Decalogues put before Israel the way of obedience to the law revealed by God on Sinai (or Horeb). The divine plan calls for a human response in the context of the Covenant (Exod 24:7-8; Deut 5:2-3).

The laws that in the Torah follow the Decalogues develop their content. The prohibition against idolatry is the *leitmotif* of Deuteronomy, while the appeal to a fraternal life is thematized in the Holiness Code (Lev 17–26) and culminates in the call to love of neighbor, that is, of both the one who is a member of the community of Israel and the resident alien (Lev 19:18, 34).

The Decalogues show how God the Creator reveals himself also as a Savior in history and invites every member of the community to enter, in turn, into this logic of salvation by putting into effect a demanding community ethic. The covenant with God the Creator and Savior leads the faithful to "live in conformity with the truth."

The Decalogues furnish an interpretive key for the whole of the Torah, and ultimately they constitute a true "catechism" for the community of Israel. This catechism enables the Israelites to affirm their faith in the one true God, confronting the challenges of history, and to engage in a fraternal communal life by renouncing schemes of power and violence. In other words, the Decalogues combine the attestation of a truth concerning God himself (he is the *Creator* and *Savior*) with a truth regarding the manner of a just and upright life. The relationship to the God of Israel turns out to be so inseparable from one's relationship to one's neighbor that this is the place *par excellence* in which the adherence of believers to the revealed truth is expressed.

2.3 The Historical Books

70. The compendium of Israel's history found in so many books of the Bible, especially the so-called historical books (Josh; Judg; 1–2 Sam; 1–2 Kgs; 1–2 Chr; Ezra; Neh; 1–2 Macc), clearly shows that the point is not to produce a historiography in the modern sense, that is, in the sense of the most objective possible chronicle of past events. Every attempt to interpret the biblical history from a modern perspective runs the risk of reading the texts without regard to their intention and failing to grasp the fullness of their meaning.

The biblical presentation of history develops harmoniously on the basis of the theology of creation, as it is presented in the first pages of the Bible (see above), insofar as it is a testimony of the experience of God and insofar as it reveals that he acts for the salvation of humanity in history (Josh 24). Consequently, biblical historiography seeks to show that the saving will of God is completely reasonable, since it is directed entirely toward the good of humanity. In biblical history it is not just positive events that are narrated; on the contrary, it is shown how, in the contradictory events of human life, God manifests his constant intention of bringing about the salvation of humanity. In this way, biblical history (Judg 6:36; 2 Sam 22:28) reveals him as the "Savior."

God's involvement with human beings, attested in the biblical account, is presented as a history of "covenants," starting from the covenant with Noah for all humanity and continuing with those which characterize the history of Israel. The covenant, which God offers to his people in the person of Abraham and then solemnly concluded with Israel at Sinai, is continually broken by the people in the course of history, so that it is solely due to the fidelity of God that the covenant comes to be called "eternal."

Consequently, the theological program of biblical historiography presents itself in the first place as theo-logy in the literal sense of the term, which seeks to show that God is faithful in his relationship with humanity. This is confirmed up until the announcement of a new covenant in Jeremiah 31:31. It is the covenant of God, who leads his people to salvation in him and with him through the events of history.

2.4 The Prophetic Books

71. Biblical prophecy attests the self-revelation of God in a remarkable way, because the human word of the prophets coincides explicitly with the Word of God: "Thus says the Lord" is, in fact, a formula typical of this literature. And an essential characteristic of such a revelation is its manifestation in human history: in events placed in a reliable chronology, in words addressed to concrete individuals by human beings whose names, origins, and dates are often known. God's eternal plan to establish a covenant of love with humanity (cf. *DV*, n. 2) is made known to the prophets (Amos 3:7) and is proclaimed by the prophets to Israel and to the nations, so that the authentic truth of God and of history is manifested to all.

From the inexhaustible riches of the prophetic word, sign of the infinite wisdom of God, several notable characteristics flow that contribute in a specific way to outline the face of the true God and promote adherence of faith.

2.4.1 The Faithful God

The prophets succeed one another in history, according to the Lord's promise: "I will raise up for them a prophet like you from among their own people; I will put my words in the mouth of the prophet, who shall speak to them everything that I command" (Deut 18:18). In the prophetic succession, the charism of Moses (Deut 18:15) is transmitted to those who, by their very appearance, become witnesses of God's fidelity to his covenant (Isa 38:18-19; 49:7), witnesses of a goodness that embraces a thousand generations (Exod 34:7; Deut 5:10; 7:9; Jer 32:18). The God who is the origin of the human event, the Father from whom life flows, does not abandon (Isa 41:17; Hos 11:8), does not forget his creatures (Isa 44:21; 54:10; Jer 31:20): "Can a woman forget her nursing child, or show no compassion for the child of her womb? Even these may forget, yet I will not forget you" (Isa 49:15).

The prophets, sent assiduously by God (Jer 7:13, 25; 11:7; 25:3-4; etc.), are the authoritative voice which recalls the unfailing presence of the true God in the turmoil of human history (Isa 41:10; 43:5; Jer 30:11). They proclaim, "You will show faithfulness to Jacob and unswerving loyalty to Abraham, as you have sworn to our ancestors from the days of old" (Mic 7:20).

The truth of the Lord is comparable, therefore, to that of a rock (Isa 26:4), fully reliable (Deut 32:4). If people hold fast to his words, they will be able to stand firm (Isa 7:9) without fear of being lost (Hos 14:10).

2.4.2 The Just God

72. Revealing himself, the faithful God demands faithfulness; the holy God requires that whoever enters into his covenant be holy as he is holy (Lev 19:2); the just God asks each person to walk the path of righteousness set out by the law (Deut 6:25). Over the

course of history, the prophets are the heralds of perfect justice, that accomplished by God (Isa 30:18; 45:21; Jer 9:3; 12:1; Zeph 3:5) and that which he urges on human beings (Isa 1:17; 5:7; 26:2; Ezek 18:5-18; Amos 5:24); they not only recall the directives of the Lord, explaining their meaning, but also courageously denounce any deviation from the path of righteousness made by individuals and nations. In this way, they call to conversion, threatening just punishment for crimes committed, and they announce inevitable disaster on those who, in their perversity, do not heed the divine warning (Isa 30:12-14; Jer 6:19; 7:13-15).

The truth of the prophetic word manifests itself most clearly here, in opposition to the easy consolation of the false prophets who, neglecting the demanding moral requirements of the law, announce peace when the sword of judgment looms (Jer 6:14; 23:17; Ezek 13:10), deceiving the people with illusory promises (Isa 9:14-15; Jer 27:14; 29:8-9; Amos 9:10; Zech 10:2), and facilitating, therefore, the continuance of iniquity. "The prophets who preceded you and me," says Jeremiah to the (false) prophet Hananiah, "prophesied war, famine, and pestilence against many countries and great kingdoms" (Jer 28:8); the authentic word of the Lord, therefore, affirms that the world's wickedness is revealed historically by the just God precisely through painful chastisement. The passage through humiliation and death is thus explained by the prophets as the necessary discipline that fosters the acknowledgment of sin (Jer 2:19) and the disposition of the penitent humbly to await forgiveness (Joel 2:12-14).

2.4.3 The Merciful God

73. A good portion of the prophetic literature takes on a threatening tone, much like that of Jonah in Nineveh (Jonah 3:4), because it announces misfortune "against all flesh" (Ezek 21:4-5), not only declaring the dissolution of the Kingdom of Israel (Jer 5:31; Hos 10:15; Amos 8:2), but even evoking the end of the world (Jer 4:23-26; 45:4; Ezek 7:2-6; Dan 8:17). This catastrophic outlook could lead one to think that God has not been faithful to his promise: "Ah, Lord GOD, how utterly you have deceived this people and Jerusalem, saying, 'It shall be well with you,' even while the sword is at the throat!"

(Jer 4:10); "Where are your zeal and your might? The yearning of your heart and your compassion?" (Isa 63:15).

The voice of the prophets who proclaim the consolation of Israel (Isa 40:1) responds to this lament, which became the prayer of a people in exile; what could have been considered a definitive end is transformed, by the power of the Creator, into a new beginning (Jer 31:22; Ezek 37:1ff.; Hos 2:16-17); what had apparently been a failure becomes the beginning of a marvelous reality, because the sin which caused the catastrophe is definitively pardoned by the mercy of the Father (Jer 31:34; Ezek 16:63; Hos 14:5; Mic 7:19).

It is the prophets who declare the radical turning point in the history of Israel (Jer 30:3, 18; 31:23; Ezek 16:53; Joel 4:1; Amos 9:14; Zeph 3:20) and in world history itself, since they announce new heavens and a new earth (Isa 65:17; 66:22; Jer 31:22). The event of divine forgiveness, accompanied by an unprecedented richness of spiritual gifts (Jer 31:33-34; Ezek 36:27; Hos 2:21-22; Joel 2:1-2) and which is rendered visible by the extraordinary flowering of a people restored in perfect institutional forms (Isa 54:1-3; 62:1-3; Jer 30:18-21; Hos 14:5-9), the definitive event in history, therefore, could not have been foreseen or imagined by the human mind: "From this time forward," says the Lord through Isaiah, "I make you hear new things, hidden things that you have not known. They are created now, not long ago; before today you have never heard of them, so that you could not say, 'I already knew them'" (Isa 48:6-7). It is the Lord, by means of the prophets, who reveals his projects, infinitely superior to what his creatures could possibly conceive (Isa 55:8-9), and it is in the effective manifestation of grace that God makes known the perfection of his truth, bringing to fulfillment the sense of history.

This word of promise is truthful precisely because it is fulfilled (Deut 18:22; Isa 14:24; 45:23; 48:3; Jer 1:12; 28:9): "For as the rain and the snow come down from heaven, and do not return there until they have watered the earth, making it bring forth and sprout, giving seed to the sower and bread to the eater, so shall my word be that goes out from my mouth; it shall not return to me empty, but it shall accomplish that which I purpose, and succeed in the thing for which I sent it" (Isa 55:10-11). The unique and epoch-making event produces an eternal covenant (Isa 55:3; Jer 32:40; Ezek 16:60). It is from here that praise, the ultimate effect of salvation, flows: "O LORD, you are my God; I will exalt you and praise your name; for you have accomplished marvels conceived from of old, faithful and true" (Isa 25:1).

Those who believe in Christ will recognize that they are descendants of the prophets and the promise (Acts 3:25), to whom the consoling word of salvation was sent (Acts 13:26): in the paschal celebration of the Lord Jesus they will experience, as they worship, the full manifestation of the faithful, just, and merciful God.

2.5 The Psalms

74. The prayers of the Psalms presuppose and make clear this essential truth about God and salvation: God is not an absolute impersonal principle but a Person who hears and responds. Every Israelite knows that he or she can turn to him in any situation of life, whether in joy or in sorrow. God revealed himself as the God who is present (see Exod 3:14), knows the one praying, and nurtures for that person the most lively and benevolent interest.

Among the various characteristics of God attested by the Psalms, we recall two: God reveals himself (a) as the God of protecting power and (b) as the God of justice who transforms the sinner into a righteous person. God is, therefore, always the One who saves human beings.

2.5.1 The Omnipotent God (Ps 46)

The presence and activity of God are manifested in a characteristic way in Psalm 46; they are expressed in the phrase "The LORD of hosts is with us" (vv. 8, 12). At the beginning, in the middle, and at the end of the psalm, the presence of God, who is "for us" and "with us," is underlined (vv. 2, 8, 12). He dominates nature by his power (vv. 2-7); he defends Israel and creates peace (vv. 8-12).

a) The Power of God Ruling Nature: God as Creator

In the face of cosmic upheavals, the people of the covenant remain calm: "God is our refuge and strength, a very present help in trouble. Therefore we will not fear, though the earth should change, though the mountains shake in the heart of the sea; though its waters roar and foam, though the mountains tremble with its tumult" (vv. 2-4). God dominates the chaotic forces. Even if they threaten the stability of Zion, the holy city "shall not be moved" (v. 5a), for "God is in the midst" (v. 5a), and "God will help it when the morning dawns" (v. 5b).

b) The Power of God Defends His People and Creates Peace: God as Savior

The declaration "The LORD of hosts is with us" appears as the response to the anguished cry of the people surrounded by enemies: "Rise up, come to our help" (Ps 44:26). God is called a "refuge and strength" (Ps 46:1) and a "bulwark" (vv. 7, 11) to indicate the power by which he protects his faithful, gathered in Zion. All are invited to recognize this: "Come, behold the works of the LORD" (v. 8). The psalm then specifies what these works are: "He makes wars cease to the end of the earth; he breaks the bow and shatters the spear; he burns shields with fire" (v. 9). The Lord himself turns to the faithful, saying, "Be still, and know that I am God! I am exalted among the nations, I am exalted on the earth" (v. 11). Adversaries must cease hostilities; they must recognize the Lord and his universal majesty, which rises above all nations and all the earth. God's powerful intervention on behalf of Zion has a universal significance: he brings peace not only to the city of God (see v. 5) but to all nations, to the whole earth (see v. 10).

2.5.2 The God of Justice (Ps 51)

75. In this psalm, the confession of sins is merged with petition. The underlying dynamism, alluded to at the center of the first and second parts of the psalm, is the justice of God: "You are justified in your sentence and blameless when you pass judgment" (v. 4); "Deliver me from bloodshed, O God, O God of my salvation, and my tongue will sing aloud of your deliverance" (v. 14; see v. 19). The salvific justice of God works in sinful human beings, not simply canceling their faults and purifying them, but also justifying and

transforming them. This entire action of the just God proceeds from his love, a love that is faithful and merciful.

a) The God of Justice Loves the Sinner

God, impelled by his love, justifies the sinner. The psalm begins with the plea: "Have mercy on me, O God, according to your steadfast love; according to your abundant mercy blot out my transgressions" (v. 1). The supplicant invokes the love and mercy of God.

The first noun, "steadfast love" (*hesed*), is one of the fundamental terms in the theology of the Psalms and the covenant (it is very frequent in the Old Testament, especially in the Psalms); it indicates that attitude of God which implies goodness, generosity, and faithfulness toward the one praying. In the Psalms, this love is often depicted as though it were a person: "Let your steadfast love and your faithfulness keep me safe forever" (Ps 40:12). God sends it from heaven (Ps 57:3; see 61:8; 85:11; 89:15) so that it might accompany believers, follow them like a friend (Ps 23:6), surround them (Ps 32:10), and satisfy them (Ps 90:14). It is more important than life itself: "Your steadfast love is better than life" (Ps 63:3; see Ps 42:8; 62:12). The love of God will not be taken away from the sinners in spite of their sin (see Ps 77:9), because God loves them as a father. This love will inspire the justice of God, which will in turn make the sinner righteous.

The second term, "mercy" (*rehem*; see Pss 40:11; 69:16; etc.), is frequently found in penitential contexts (see Pss 25:6; 79:8) and is usually used in the plural (*rahamim*). It evokes the "womb" of a mother, the archetypal symbol of an instinctive and radical love. God is depicted as being even more attached to the human person than a mother is to her child (see Isa 49:15). For this reason, the psalmist says: "But you, O Lord, are a God merciful and gracious, slow to anger and abounding in steadfast love and faithfulness" (Ps 86:15).

In reality, the two terms, which in a certain sense describe two types of divine love (paternal and maternal), are combined: "Be mindful of your mercy, O LORD, and your steadfast love, for they have been from of old" (Ps 25:6; see 103:13). God loves humankind—even if they are sinners—as a mother loves her child, with a love that is not the fruit of merit but entirely gratuitous, with a love that is a fundamental need of the heart. At the same time, God loves them as a father: with a generous and faithful love. The two dimensions of God's love, evoked at the beginning of Psalm 51, are like two dimensions of his justice, which makes the sinner righteous. The God who loves and is merciful (v. 1; see v. 18) is at the same time the God who judges (v. 4; see v. 16).

b) The Justice of God Justifies, That Is, Transforms the Sinner into a Righteous Person (vv. 6, 16)

76. Approaching the sinner, God establishes with him a dynamic and profound relationship, inspired by justice. This process unfolds in various stages:

- Compassion or loving mercy. "Have mercy on me, O God" (v. 1). Here, the verb "to be gracious" (*hanan*) is used (see Pss 4:1; 6:2; etc.); it indicates a graceful "bending down" of the sovereign toward the subject. The one who rebelled against God and became an abomination in his sight asks to know his compassion. It will raise the sinner from the deepest misery—that caused by sin.

- Interior teaching. "You desire truth in the inward being; therefore teach me wisdom in my secret heart" (v. 6). God acts within the sinner's conscience, darkened by sin, and inserts into it the light of truth, which leads to the recognition of sins, and the enlightenment of his wisdom, which opens the eyes to right conduct.

- The verdict of grace which grants pardon. The sinner, confined to the domain of sin, recognizes: "You are justified in your sentence" (v. 4). The sinner's invocations, "blot out . . . wash . . . cleanse" (vv. 1-2, repeated in vv. 7-10), give way to a strong hope: "Hide your face from my sins, and blot out all my iniquities" (v. 9). Freed from sin's obsessive presence, the sinner pleads: "Let me hear joy and gladness" (v. 8; see Isa 66:14).

- The new creation. The sinner asks for a new creation from God: "Create in me a clean heart, O God" (v. 10). After this fundamental request, he begs three times to receive the Spirit:

"a new and right spirit," the presence of "your holy spirit," "a willing spirit" (vv. 10-12). An interior and permanent renewal is sought, for which the presence of the Spirit of God, from whom "the joy of your salvation" comes (v. 12), is decisive.

• The urge to witness. Human beings, renewed by God, wish to communicate their experience to all those who have need of it: "Then I will teach transgressors your ways" (v. 13). Above all, they wish to teach them that wisdom which was inculcated within them by God.

• The openness to joy and praise. The renewed penitent feels pervaded by joy and wishes to express it in praise: "my tongue will sing aloud of your deliverance. O Lord, open my lips, and my mouth will declare your praise" (vv. 14-15; see Pss 35:28; 71:24).

• The parallelism between "your justice" and "your praise" in the final verses leads to the conclusion that God's justice does not generate fear. On the contrary, God himself, motivated by his paternal and maternal love, is the sole cause of achieving the justification of the sinner, that is, the new creation and happiness of the sinner, liberated from the oppression of sin.

2.6 The Song of Songs

77. It is surprising that the Song of Songs was accepted into the Hebrew Bible (among the "five scrolls"); its content is, in fact, completely unique. Recognized as an inspired text and integrated into the Christian canon, it has given rise to a unique Christological interpretation. The Song is a poem which celebrates marital love, that which is the fullness of human experience, that love which consists in a mutual seeking and a personal communion between man and woman. This seeking and communion bear within themselves a fascinating and boundless dynamism which transforms two human creatures, a shepherd and a young woman, into a king and a queen, a royal couple.

The Song poetically celebrates human love, real love, in its physical and, at the same time, spiritual dimensions. But it does so in a form that is open to a more mysterious and theological dimension. The text has several layers of meaning: to the basic meaning of human love, further meanings are added, always rooted in spousal love, which is, so to speak, the symbol of every other form of love. The first additional meaning regards the love of God for every human person. The poem, founded on the affirmation that "God created humankind in his image" (Gen 1:27), sings of the passionate love between a man and a woman as an image of the passionate and personal love of God. The love of God for every human creature (cf. Wis 11:26) bears within itself all the characteristics of masculine love (of the groom, the husband, and the father) and, at the same time, those of feminine love (of the bride, the wife, and the mother). Authentic human love is a symbol through which the Creator reveals himself to humankind as the God who is love (see 1 John 4:7, 8, 16). Using many symbols, the book makes us realize that God is the source of human love. He creates it, nurtures it, makes it grow, gives it the strength to seek the other and to live with him or her, ultimately with the family or the community in perfect communion. That is why all human love (considered in itself, not simply as a metaphor) contains a divine seed and energy. By knowing love and living it, therefore, one can discover and know God. Moreover, through human love, man and woman are touched by the love of God himself (see 1 John 4:17). And by remaining in love, they enter into communion with God (see 1 John 4:12).

The second additional meaning regards the love of God for the people of the covenant (cf. Hos 1–3; Ezek 16, 23; Isa 5:1-7; 62:5; Jer 2-3). It finds a new actuality and is fulfilled in the love of Christ for the Church. Christ presents himself or is presented as the bridegroom in different contexts (Mark 2:19; John 3:29; 2 Cor 11:2; Eph 5:25, 29; Rev 19:7, 9; 21:2, 9), and the Church is portrayed as the fiancée (Rev 19:7, 9) who becomes the bride in the eschatological fulfillment (Rev 21:9). The love of Christ for the Church is so important and fundamental for the salvation of humankind that the Gospel of John presents what Jesus did at the wedding at Cana as the beginning of his signs (John 2:11) and of his ministry as a whole. Jesus reveals himself as the true bridegroom (John 3:29) who procures the good wine in abundance for all and reveals this love which he will give "to the end" (John 13:1; cf. 10:11, 15; 15:13; 17:23, 26).

2.7 The Wisdom Literature

78. The wisdom texts also display various characteristics of the Creator God, in particular those of the merciful and inscrutable God. The Creator, in fact, is the merciful God who forgets the sins of men and women with a view to their conversion. On the other hand, he is mysterious and inscrutable; human beings must recognize their own limits as creatures, walking in the way of faithfulness without being able to discern the reason for what God accomplishes in history. We will underline here some aspects of wisdom which illustrate the authenticity of God's truth: it seeks to lead human beings to the adherence of faith in the Lord and seeks to arouse in them "the fear of the Lord," that is, a profound respect, conscious of the immense distance that exists between the Creator and his creatures (Eccl 3:10-14).

2.7.1 Wisdom and Sirach: The Philanthropy of God

a) The Book of Wisdom

79. The philanthropy of God, communicated in Wisdom 11:15–12:27, is expressed above all in the memory of the so-called plagues which struck the Egyptians, interpreting in an innovative way the punishments of God and his pedagogy. The God of the covenant, the lord of creation (Wis 16:24-29; 19:6-21), intervening repeatedly in salvation history, takes care of his people, as of every "just person" (3:1–4:19). It is he who rewards and punishes (4:20–5:23; 11:1-5), treating everyone with forbearance in order to bring them to conversion (12:9-18; cf. Rom 2:3-4; 2 Pet 3:9) and to educate the just to judge with clemency (Wis 12:19-22).

Having recalled that God, at the time of the Exodus, punished with moderation the enemies of his people, the author explains the reasons for such behavior. Although recognizing the fact that there was no difficulty for "your all-powerful hand, which created the world out of formless matter" (Wis 11:17), the author adds: "You are merciful to all, for you can do all things, and you overlook people's sins, so that they may repent" (Wis 11:23; cf. Pss 103:8-12; 130:3-4; Exod 34:6-7). Moderation toward Egypt (Wis 11:15–12:2) is not a sign of weakness; rather, God acted in this way out of "compassion toward all" and because he wishes to lead everyone to conversion so that, renouncing their wickedness, they might arrive at faith in him: "Therefore you correct little by little those who trespass, and you remind and warn them of the things through which they sin, so that they may be freed from wickedness and put their trust in you, O Lord" (12:2). The omnipotence of God is revealed not in his might but, on the contrary, in his mercy. The power of God is the source not of judgment but of forgiveness (cf. Sir 18:7-12; Rom 2:4). It is precisely the omnipotence itself of God which motivates his compassion. The mercy of God also manifests itself in the way in which he punishes the inhabitants of the land (Wis 12:8): he treats them kindly, with clemency (cf. 11:26), because they are fragile human beings (cf. Ps 78:39). If God used forbearance in punishing them and pardoned them, it was not through impotence or because he ignored their crimes (Wis 12:11).

The author does not stop here, offering us one of the most beautiful insights of the entire Old Testament: "For you love all things that exist, and detest none of the things that you have made, for you would not have made anything if you had hated it. . . . You spare all things, for they are yours, O Lord, you who love the living" (11:24, 26). God cannot fail to love what he himself has formed, because his incorruptible Spirit is in all things (cf. 1:7; 12:1). God created everything in order to save it; he has compassion on all with a view to their conversion and does not wish to destroy anything of what he has created (11:26).

The love of God manifests itself even in the premature death of the righteous. He loves the righteous for their virtues as well as for their immaculate life (4:9), and he removes them from this perverse world lest they be corrupted: "There were some who pleased God and were loved by him, and while living among sinners were taken up" (Wis 4:10; cf. Gen 5:24; Sir 44:16; Heb 11:5).

The love of God for his creatures is not a static but a dynamic love; it reveals itself in action. The fact that creatures continue in existence and conserve their multifaceted, active, mysterious being are the most tangible proofs of God's love in action.

b) The Book of Sirach

80. Ben Sira too has a vivid sense of the greatness of God as omnipotence and mercy. He speaks of God with moving enthusiasm and wonder. God is omnipotent, and in his providence he grants wisdom to the scribe (Sir 37:21; 39:6) and the success which derives from it (10:5), and he also gives riches to the poor (11:12–13:21). From him also comes the decree of death for each person (41:4). God's mercy stands out alongside his greatness: "To none has he given power to proclaim his works; and who can search out his mighty deeds?" (18:4). Because of the fragility of creatures made of flesh and blood, earth and dust, God has been patient with humanity, pouring out his mercy (18:10) on "all flesh" (Sir 18:13; cf. Wis 11:21–12:18; Ps 145:9). This divine indulgence must not be used to take away human responsibility; it is, rather, an invitation to conversion: "Turn back to the Lord and forsake your sins; pray in his presence and lessen your offense. Return to the Most High and turn away from iniquity, and hate intensely what he abhors" (Sir 17:25-26).

2.7.2 Job and Ecclesiastes: The Inscrutability of God

a) The Book of Job

81. The book of Job, framed by a double prologue (1:1–2:13) and a double epilogue (42:7-17), is a long dialogue through which one moves from a "known" God to the revelation of an unpredictable and mysterious God.

Job had ardently desired the presence of the Lord (9:32-35; 13:22-24; 16:19-22; 23:3-5; 30:20); he had even demanded a response from God (31:35), because he wanted to discuss his case directly with him. But it was an error for Job to confront God, dealing with him as if he were his equal. By challenging the way

God works, demanding an account of his actions, Job in some sense makes himself equal to his Creator. It is impossible for him to attain the infinite heights of the Omnipotent God, whose perfection is inaccessible to the human mind (11:7). To express in an eloquent and poetic way the divine transcendence which surpasses all human understanding, the heavens, the underworld, the earth, and the sea are all presented as symbols of cosmic height, profundity, length, and width, all of them exceeded by the divine immensity (11:8-9). The profundity of the divine mystery leaves the human being ignorant and powerless (cf. Amos 9:1-4; Jer 23:24; Deut 30:11-14; Eph 3:18-21). In fact, it is given to human beings to touch the limits of human greatness; the prophets had already stigmatized those "who are wise in their own eyes and clever in their own sight" (Isa 5:21; cf. Isa 10:13; 19:12; 29:14; Jer 8:8-9; 9:22-23; Ezek 28).

Although God does not respond to any of Job's questions, in the end he utters a beautiful discourse in chapters 38–41 of the book. In a grand theophany in the form of a storm, he finally speaks, not to reply to those who had spoken, but to put Job through a kind of interrogation, to direct him toward the mystery of his person. In his discourse, a number of questions follow one another rapidly, accompanied occasionally by extensive descriptions. God makes Job aware of his ignorance, his limits as a creature, while the wisdom of the Creator has no limits (cf. Job 28). A clear affirmation underlies all of God's questions: God is present in his creation, which, in its infinite variety, remains a mystery to humans. The human criteria of judgment are not adequate for confronting the mysteries of creation.

Job had known God by hearsay (42:5), according to the traditional form of a theology based on the rigid principle of retribution. After God's lengthy discourse, he finally knows God in a more adequate way. At the end of his struggle, he confesses: "I know that you can do all things; no purpose of yours can be thwarted. You asked, 'Who is this that obscures my plans without knowledge?' Surely I spoke of things I did not understand, things too wonderful for me to know" (42:2-3). Job has found his place and is able to discover both the grandeur of God and the inaccessibility of his omnipotence. His encounter with God revealed to him the futility of demanding to put God on trial. He remains a man who suffers, but without pretensions. At the end, he finds himself again; he accepts that he is only dust and thus becomes more humble, more human (42:6). Job realizes that the human being cannot know the designs of God, but in the end he understands that his eyes have seen God himself through what he does in the world (42:5). Observing the universe and humanity with the eyes of God, he is able to confess the error of his outlook: he went too far; for this reason he says, "I repent" (42:6a). For Job, wisdom now consists in confessing that God can be recognized as just without being totally understood and that one can commit oneself in fidelity to him without knowing "from the beginning to the end" (Eccl 3:11) the meaning of what God has done. God remains an unfathomable mystery for human beings.

b) The Book of Ecclesiastes (Qoheleth)

82. The author of this book (in Hebrew, *Qoheleth*) develops further the theme of God's inscrutable activity. Adopting the point of view of the wise (Eccl 8:16-17), he sets out in search of the meaning of life insofar as it is made visible in the real world, on earth and under the sun. The sage wishes to understand the meaning of the frantic pursuits of human beings on earth (8:16) and asserts: "I saw all the work of God, that no one can find out what is happening under the sun. However much they may toil in seeking, they will not find it out" (8:17; cf. Job 42:3). No human beings can ever modify what God has accomplished in their time (cf. Eccl 1:15; 3:1-8, 14; 6:10; 7:13). God prevented human beings from knowing his own work (Eccl 7:13-14; cf. Job 9:2-4). Qoheleth takes up this theme again in 11:5, where the work of God is described as incomprehensible and is compared to the mystery of pregnancy in the maternal womb. The human being is ignorant of the meaning of life, but in the will of God all created things have their own place and their own time (Eccl 3:11). The secret of God's work is inaccessible, unfathomable, and incomprehensible to those who seek its meaning based on their own experience. Both the work of God and God himself, the Creator, remain for human beings an inscrutable mystery.

2.8 Conclusion

83. The testimony of biblical wisdom reveals to all the authentic truth of God who is merciful; at the same time, he presents himself as an unfathomable mystery to human beings. The benevolence of God leads human beings to conversion and to faith, while the inscrutability of God leads them to recognize the greatness of the Creator and their own limitations, to have the "fear of the Lord" and to observe his commandments.

We note that the approaches to the truth about God in the books of Wisdom and Sirach, on the one hand, and in Job and Ecclesiastes, on the other, are very different. According to the first two books, truth may be reached by means of reason and/or through the knowledge of the Torah, while the books of Job and Ecclesiastes insist on the human incapacity to understand the mystery of God and his activity: there remains only the trust that believers have in God himself, even though they do not comprehend the logic of events and of the world itself.

The New Testament changes the perspective of the reflection and shows that truth goes beyond the understanding of Israelite wisdom and manifests itself fully and definitively in the person of Christ.

III. The Testimony of Select New Testament Texts

84. In the New Testament, we can distinguish the gospels from the apostolic letters and the book of Revelation because of their specific literary genres. This subdivision also governs our presentation relating to the truth attested in these books.

3.1 The Gospels

Among the books of the Christian Bible, a preeminent place belongs to the gospels, written testimony of the divine revelation at its culminating point; in them, in fact, we find the self-revelation of God the Father through his Son, who, having become human, lived, suffered and died, and raised our human nature to the divine glory through his resurrection. The Dogmatic Constitution *Dei Verbum* affirms, "The profound truth, about God and the salvation of human beings . . . shines for us in Christ" (n. 2). From here, the Constitution draws the consequence "that among all the Scriptures, even those of the New Testament, the Gospels have a special pre-eminence, and rightly so, for they are the principal witness of the life and teaching of the incarnate Word, our Savior" (n. 18). The same conciliar text also affirms the apostolic origin of the four gospels (n. 18): the apostles, as "eyewitnesses and ministers of the word" (Luke 1:2), and their disciples link the Church with Christ himself through the written testimony of the gospels.

Moreover, *Dei Verbum* reiterates the historical character of the gospels; these "faithfully hand on what Jesus Christ, while living among men, really did and taught for their eternal salvation" (n. 19). It then describes the process which led to the composition of the four gospels: they are not to be reduced to the status of symbolic, mythical, poetic creations of anonymous authors, but are a reliable account of events in the life and ministry of Jesus. It would be wrong to expect an exact equivalence between every single element of the text and the details of the events, since this does not correspond to the nature and intention of the gospels. The diverse factors which modify the accounts and create differences between them do not prevent a reliable presentation of the events. Likewise considered erroneous is the assumption which theorizes the discontinuity between Jesus and the traditions which attest him, or the lack of interest or the incapacity to present him in an adequate way. The gospels, therefore, establish a real link with the true Jesus.

3.2 The Synoptic Gospels

85. We will now examine, first in the Synoptic Gospels and then in the Gospel of John, the truth which Christ reveals about God and about human salvation. Obviously it is impossible to give a complete picture; we must content ourselves, therefore, with a few indications.

3.2.1 The Truth about God

In Matthew 11:27 (cf. Luke 10:22), Jesus says, "All things have been handed over to me by my Father; and no one knows the Son except the Father, and no one knows the Father except the Son and anyone to whom the Son chooses to reveal him." Jesus asserts an exclusive relationship of reciprocal knowledge between himself and God. God knows Jesus as his own Son (Matt 3:17; 17:5; Luke 3:22; 9:35), and Jesus knows God as his own Father, with whom he enjoys an absolutely unique relationship. This knowledge of the Father is the basis for the unique capacity of Jesus to reveal God, to make known his true aspect. And his revelation of God as Father always implies the revelation of himself as Son. From this unique capacity of Jesus, the primary task of his mission, the revelation of God, derives. Not simply the words, but also the deeds and the entire way of Jesus reveal God and demand continuous and vigilant attention to this revelation.

Jesus reveals God as the Father of his listeners in a particularly explicit way in the Gospel of Matthew. This happens especially in the Sermon on the Mount (Matt 5–7). There Jesus makes known to his listeners that their Father knows what they need before they ask for it (6:8) and teaches them to turn to God calling him "Our Father in heaven" (6:9). He instructs them on his watchful concern, which renders human anxieties superfluous (6:25-34). The Father, who is generous toward the good and the bad (5:45), is the model for their actions: "Be perfect, therefore, as your heavenly Father is perfect" (5:48). Only "the one who does the will of my Father in heaven" (7:21), says Jesus, treads the right path and escapes the final disaster (cf. 7:24-27). Those who hear Jesus are "the light of the world" (5:14) and have the task of making the Father known through their good works, so that people "might give glory to your Father in heaven" (5:16). Revealing the Father, Jesus also assigns the mission of making the Father known.

In the Gospel of Luke, Jesus, in revealing the Father, highlights above all the mercy of God toward sinners. He expresses this quality of God in a marvelous way in the parable of the father who has two sons; he receives with compassion and joy the one who was lost but seeks to convince the one who remained at home (Luke 15:11-32). With this parable, Jesus explains and justifies his attitude toward sinners (cf. Luke 15:1-10). At the end of the episode with the publican Zacchaeus, he asserts: "For the Son of Man came to seek out and to save the lost" (19:10). He thus presents the core of his mission, and manifests the will and activity of God the Father.

The way Mark describes the beginning of Jesus' public ministry is significant and programmatic: "Now after John was arrested, Jesus came to Galilee, proclaiming the good news of God, and saying, 'The time is fulfilled, and the kingdom of God has come near; repent, and believe in the good news'" (1:14-15). The content of Jesus' proclamation is "the Gospel of God," the good news which speaks of God and comes from God. Jesus comes as the revealer of God, and his revelation is good news. He proclaims that the Kingdom of God has drawn near. The reality of the "Kingdom of God" is at the heart of Jesus' preaching in the Synoptic Gospels. It reveals and underlines the royal sovereignty of God, his pastoral concern for all, his active and powerful intervention in human history. Through all his activity, Jesus explains and makes explicit this truth about God.

3.2.2 The Truth about Human Salvation

86. The human being is a creature of God for whom Jesus, the Son of God, is an ever-valid model of gratitude, obedience, and openness to God the Father, who is the source of all salvation.

The healing of the sick and liberation of those possessed by demons represent an essential part of Jesus' ministry. Matthew places the same summary at the outset (4:23) and conclusion (9:35) of the great beginning of Jesus' activity (5:1–9:34) which, in the second part, sets forth a series of his marvelous interventions (8:1–9:34). In this summary, two works of Jesus are mentioned: the announcement of the Kingdom and the healing of "every disease and every sickness among the people" (4:23). This activity exposes the infirmities and the needs of human beings, as well as the generous and powerful ability of Jesus to overcome such misery. The herald of the Kingdom of God brings about health of body efficaciously, showing the compassion of God for his suffering creature and his will to save him or her. This activity of Jesus is received with enthusiasm; Matthew says: "They brought to him all the sick, those who were afflicted with various diseases and pains, demoniacs, epileptics, and paralytics, and he cured them" (4:24). In many stories, it is evident that

Jesus does not impose healing, but presupposes the faith of those who come to him (cf. Matt 8:10; 9:22, 28; 15:28). The report on his visit to Nazareth concludes with the observation: "And he did not do many deeds of power there, because of their unbelief" (Matt 13:58). The healings are real and have great significance, but they do not constitute the objective of Jesus' ministry. Already before his birth, the angel explains to Joseph the meaning of the name of Jesus: "You are to name him Jesus, for he will save his people from their sins" (Matt 1:21). Illnesses are not the greatest misery experienced by human beings but sins, that is, the relationship with God and with one's neighbor that has been altered and broken. Human beings are incapable of breaking free from this miserable state; they need a powerful Savior to reconcile them with God. The name "Jesus" signifies "The Lord saves"; God sent the Savior of Israel and of all humanity in the person of his Son Jesus. Jesus draws near to sinners not as a judge but as a physician full of mercy, to heal them, and he calls them to conversion (Matt 9:12-13). He gives "his life a ransom for many" (Matt 20:28; Mark 10:45). His blood is the "blood of the covenant, which is poured out for many for the forgiveness of sins" (Matt 26:28). The sacrifice of his life ratifies the new and definitive covenant of God with Israel and with humanity, the reconciliation of God with all human beings. This is a free gift of God. To accept this invitation and be saved, or to refuse it and be lost, is the free decision of humankind (cf. Matt 22:1-13; 25:1-13, 14-30).

The Gospel of Luke describes in an incisive way what the salvation is which God gives through his Son. At the birth of Jesus, an angel of the Lord proclaims: "I am bringing you good news of great joy: . . . to you is born this day in the city of David a Savior, who is the Messiah, the Lord" (2:10-11). The Evangelist then narrates all the activity and the path of Jesus up to the crucifixion. This is followed by the repeated mocking of the Savior and Christ, who is not capable of saving himself (23:35-39). At the end, however, one of the criminals who were crucified with him (23:33) repents of his wicked deeds and expresses his faith in Jesus and in the Kingdom announced by him (23:40-42). And Jesus responds to him: "Truly I tell you, today you will be with me in Paradise" (23:43). To the repentant criminal, Jesus promises full salvation, that is, immediate communion with God, which includes the forgiveness of sins and victory over death. The appearances of the risen Jesus (24:1-53) highlight and confirm that Christ has entered into his glory (cf. 24:26) and that he, in fact, is the Savior, capable of giving the salvation promised to the crucified criminal.

We underline once more the universal character of the salvation revealed and brought about by Jesus. His mission is directed first to the people of Israel (Matt 15:24; cf. 10:6), but it is destined for all peoples. His Gospel is proclaimed in every part of the world (Matt 24:14; 26:13; cf. Mark 14:9), and his disciples are sent to all the nations (Matt 28:19; cf. Luke 24:47). God has sent Jesus as Savior of all humankind.

3.3 The Gospel of John

87. In this gospel, we find a very close connection between the truth about God and the truth about the salvation of humankind. In John 3:16, Jesus says: "For God so loved the world that he gave his only Son, so that everyone who believes in him may not perish but may have eternal life." God sends his Son to save all human beings, but in this very sending he makes himself known, revealing his relationship with the Son and his love for the world. For human beings, an intrinsic correlation is thus determined between their knowledge of God and their salvation. Jesus states, in fact, in relation to eternal life, in which full salvation consists: "This is eternal life, that they may know you, the only true God, and Jesus Christ whom you have sent" (17:3). The mediator is Jesus, the Word of God and Son of God become flesh (1:14). He reveals the Father (1:18) and brings salvation to all human beings; or rather, by revealing the Father, he reveals salvation. Let us consider now the role of Jesus under three aspects: the relationship of the Son with the Father; the relationship of the Son and Savior with humanity; the access of human beings to salvation.

3.3.1 The Son's Relationship with the Father

88. The fundamental and most characteristic feature of the relationship between the Son and the Father is their perfect unity;

Jesus says, "The Father and I are one" (10:30), and, "The Father is in me and I am in the Father" (10:38; cf. 17:21, 23). This union is expressed as an intimate reciprocal knowledge and as sublime love: "The Father knows me and I know the Father," Jesus asserts (10:15); the Father loves the Son (3:35; 5:20; 10:17; 15:9; 17:23, 24, 26), and the Son loves the Father (14:31).

We should note immediately, therefore, that the union, knowledge, and love which characterize the relationship between the Father and the Son are the foundation and model for the relationship between the Son and human beings. Jesus prays and asks the Father: "That they may all be one. As you, Father, are in me and I am in you, may they also be in us" (17:21; cf. 17:22-23). Presenting himself as the Good Shepherd, Jesus says, "I know my own and my own know me, just as the Father knows me and I know the Father" (10:14-15). It is also for love that he asserts the same connection and communication: "As the Father has loved me, so I have loved you; abide in my love. . . . This is my commandment, that you love one another as I have loved you" (15:9, 12; cf. 13:34). The Son's love derives from the love of the Father, and the love of the disciples should be rooted in the love they received from the Son and reflect the nature and intensity of that love. The Father remains the origin of it all. What the Son communicates comes from the Father and makes the Father known; it is not simply a gift from the Father but also truth about the Father, which becomes the model for human actions.

The perfect union between the Father and the Son does not signify an identity of roles. The Son is the one who receives everything from the Father; Jesus affirms that he receives life, works, and words in particular from the Father. He says: "For just as the Father has life in himself, so he has granted the Son also to have life in himself" (5:26; cf. 6:57). The Son depends on the Father for works as well: "The Son can do nothing on his own, but only what he sees the Father doing" (5:19). And Jesus often says that his teaching and words come from the Father: "The one who sent me is true, and I declare to the world what I have I heard from him. . . . I speak these things as the Father instructed me" (8:26, 28; cf. 7:16). Jesus concludes his public activity with this declaration: "I have not spoken on my own, but the Father who sent me has himself given me a commandment about what to say and what to speak. And I know that his commandment is eternal life. What I speak, therefore, I speak just as the Father has told me" (12:49-50).

The salvific orientation of this multifaceted dependence of the Son on the Father is clear. Through the life he has in himself, the Son, according to the Father's will, raises the dead on the last day (6:39-40). The words that he heard from the Father are the teaching that Jesus communicates to us (cf. 7:16; 17:8, 14). The works that he learns from the Father are the signs which make up the core of his activity and which, written and handed down in the gospel, are the basis for the faith of future generations (20:30-31). It appears clear, then, that we cannot deal with the relationship between the Father and the Son without considering the significance of this relationship for the salvation of humankind; it seems clear that the relationship between the Father and the Son has an intrinsic salvific quality.

Based on what has been seen so far, it is not possible to separate the Father and the Son, nor their intimate reciprocal relationship from the saving work of the Son. In the Gospel of John, Jesus does not speak of the Father apart from the Son; on the other hand, he does not speak of human salvation apart from the intimate relationship of the Father and the Son. He says, "Whoever has seen me has seen the Father" (14:9; cf. 12:45), and, "This is indeed the will of my Father, that all who see the Son and believe in him may have eternal life" (6:40). The truth about God and the truth about human salvation are inseparably connected to each other.

3.3.2 The Relationship of the Son and Savior with Humankind

89. On the basis of what has already been demonstrated, we find in John's gospel further clarifications about the salvific work of the Son and, consequently, about human salvation. John the Baptist introduces Jesus in his first public manifestation with these words: "Here is the Lamb of God who takes away the sin of the world" (1:29; cf. 1:36; Matt 1:21). The Samaritans understand that this man "is truly the Savior of the world" (4:42). His being lifted up on the

cross is fundamental for the salvific work of Jesus. In the sublime affirmation "I am," Jesus reveals, in a noteworthy manner, the salvific perspective, in its diverse aspects.

Already in his conversation with Nicodemus, he asserts, "And just as Moses lifted up the serpent in the wilderness, so must the Son of Man be lifted up, that whoever believes in him may have eternal life" (3:14-15). In another passage, he says: "When you have lifted up the Son of Man, then you will realize that I am he" (8:28); that is, men and women will understand his true identity as the presence of God. In relation to himself lifted up on the cross, Jesus also says: "I will draw all people to myself" (12:32). He will be the grain of wheat "that falls into the earth" which, by dying, "bears much fruit" (12:24). His lifting up is at the same time his glorification (cf. 12:23, 28; 17:1, 5), that is, the full revelation both of his love for the Father, expressed in obedience to his sending and to the will of the Father (14:31; cf. 4:34), and of the boundless love which the Father demonstrates in sending and handing over his Son to save the world (3:16). In accepting the hour determined by the Father, Jesus pushes his love for his own to the utmost, "to the end" (13:1). And his last word preceding his death on the cross is this: "It is finished!" (19:30). By dying on the cross, Jesus brought to completion the work which the Father entrusted to him for the salvation of humankind; he revealed his love—and the love of the Father—for humanity not only in words but also in deeds.

Having been sent by the Father and having received everything from the Father, Jesus reveals the salvific significance of his person, especially in the sayings which begin with "I am." With this expression—to be understood in the light of God's revelation to Moses, "I AM WHO I AM" (Exod 3:14)—Jesus asserts that God the Father is present in his person, and, at the same time, he concretizes the salvific effect of such a presence. Jesus uses the expression "I am" without any complement three times: when he walks on the waters (John 6:20), in relation to himself lifted up on the cross (8:28), and in the solemn assertion, "Very truly, I tell you, before Abraham was, I am" (8:58), always affirming his salvific presence based on his perfect union with the Father. On seven other occasions, however, the phrase "I am" is specified by a complement which introduces fundamental realities of human life. We can only briefly indicate the significance of these declarations.

In the first, Jesus asserts, "I am the bread of life" (6:35, 48, 51). We add immediately that the term "life" occurs explicitly in two other declarations (11:25; 14:6) and is implicitly present in all. Earthly life is the fundamental good, the basis for all other goods. Jesus reveals that eternal life, which consists in the most alive and complete union with God (cf. 17:3), is the highest good, is perfect salvation. The word of Jesus about the bread contains three double assertions: (a) Bread preserves you in your earthly life. From me, you receive life eternal. (b) You depend on bread (food) to be able to live; without bread, life is ended. You depend on me to obtain eternal life; you cannot give yourselves this life by yourselves. (c) To be able to live, you must eat bread. Whoever does not eat dies. To have eternal life, you must believe in me; whoever does not believe perishes.

The other words with which Jesus defines the nature of his person are structured in a similar way to that just described, and they coincide with respect to their salvific meaning. They are often connected with one of his signs and/or are found within one of his extensive instructions; the context clarifies their meaning.

The next statement is: "I am the light of the world. Whoever follows me will never walk in darkness but will have the light of life" (8:12; cf. 9:5; 12:35). Walking in darkness without having light is extremely dangerous. Jesus knows the true goal (cf. 8:14): the Father. He follows the right path and shows it to his disciples. With the following statement, "I am the gate" (10:7, 9), Jesus asserts that he gives access *to* the sheep (10:7): the true and authentic pastors of the people of God are only those whom Jesus has designated and who come in his name (cf. 21:15-17). And Jesus is also the gate *for* the sheep: only through him do the faithful find good and plentiful food to have life in abundance (10:10). Another statement of Jesus belongs to the same parabolic context: "I am the good shepherd" (10:11, 14); this expression highlights Jesus' watchful care for his own, which goes up to the giving of his own life and is characterized by a reciprocal intimacy (10:14-18).

The statement "I am the resurrection and the life" (11:25) expresses Jesus' role in the overcoming of death. In the following statement Jesus says: "I am the way, the truth, and the life. No one comes to the Father except through me" (14:6). This indicates in summary fashion the role of Jesus in giving access to God the Father, the only source of salvation and of life; it also expresses his role in reaching the Father, in knowing the Father, in participating in the Father's life. The final statement, "I am the vine, you are the branches" (15:5; cf. 15:1), sums up in a certain sense the relationship between Jesus and human beings; only if they remain in the vine can the branches live and bear fruit. The question, "What must one do, then, to be united to Jesus?" brings us to the following considerations.

3.3.3 Human Access to Salvation

90. Together with the vine, Jesus indicates two means of union with him (his words and his love): "If you abide in me, and my words abide in you" (15:7), and "Abide in my love" (15:9). The words of Jesus comprise the entire revelation brought by him. They have their origin in the Father (cf. 14:10; 17:8) and remain in whoever accepts them and believes in Jesus (cf. 12:44-50). And this is the core of the faith: "Believe me that I am in the Father and the Father is in me" (14:11). One remains in the love of Jesus, then, by welcoming him with deep gratitude and having full trust in him but also by observing his commandment "that you love one another as I have loved you" (15:12; cf. 13:34). To believe in Jesus' words and in his love and to love others are the ways to remain in him, to maintain union with him who is the vine, that is, the source of all life and salvation (cf. 1 John 3:23).

It is in the context of the final "I am" statement that Jesus says, "I have called you friends, because I have made known to you every-thing that I have heard from my Father" (15:15). His relationship with the disciples corresponds to his relationship with the Father and is by nature perfectly personal, familiar, and cordial. Remaining in this relationship with Jesus constitutes eternal life, the salvation revealed by Jesus. Jesus shows how ardently he desires such a union at the end of his great prayer to the Father; from "I am asking" (17:9, 15, 20) he passes to the singular and unheard-of "I desire," saying, "Father, I desire that those also, whom you have given me, may be with me where I am, to see my glory, which you have given me because you loved me before the foundation of the world" (17:24). The fact that the revelation of God is focused on God himself and on human salvation (cf. *Dei Verbum*, n. 2) is manifested, therefore, in a unique way in the Gospel of John.

3.4 The Letters of the Apostle Paul

91. The letters of Paul are the oldest writings in the New Testament; they relate the truth which God revealed to Israel and which, with the sending of the Son of God, Jesus Christ, was brought to completion and announced beyond the confines of the chosen people, in such a way that "there is no longer Jew or Greek" (Gal 3:28). Unlike the gospels, all later than his letters, Paul considers not so much the past as the actualization and the future of the life in Christ of the Christian communities founded either by him or by others, but all united by the same response of faith and of love.

The historical memories of Jesus that can be obtained from his letters are rather limited. And it should also be noted that in his writings, the titles attributed by the evangelists to the earthly Jesus (master, rabbi, prophet, son of David, son of man) are absent, while those prevail which directly characterize the risen one as Lord (Phil 2:11), Christ (with the tendency to be used as the proper name of Jesus; cf. Rom 5:6, 8; etc.), Son of God (Rom 1:4; Gal 4:4; etc.), image of God (2 Cor 4:4), and others. The Lord's death and resurrection, and their saving effects, constitute almost exclusively the focus of the personal and pastoral interests of Paul. He lives "by faith in the Son of God, who loved me and gave himself up for me" (Gal 2:20). He fights fiercely, therefore, against those who deform this "truth of the Gospel" (Gal 2:5), and he even opposes "Cephas" (Gal 2:11). Paul, in a certain sense, begins where the gospels end.

We will set out the testimony of Paul on God and on human salvation in four steps: (1) Paul knows revelation from his own call and from the tradition of the Church; (2) God reveals himself in Christ crucified and risen; (3) salvation is received and lived in the Church, the body of Christ; (4) the fullness of salvation consists in resurrection with Christ.

3.4.1 Paul Knows Revelation from His Own Call and from the Church's Tradition

92. Connecting his own call with what was already being preached and lived in the Church, which he had previously severely persecuted (1 Cor 15:9; Gal 1:13; Phil 3:6), Paul places himself in continuity with the tradition and with the common faith of the churches. Conscious of the unique communication, personally received, of the truth of the Gospel (Gal 1:11-17; 1 Cor 15:8), he nevertheless feels the need to share it with all the other Christian communities. Paul's relationship with believers in Christ is not simply that of a father who gives (1 Cor 4:15; Gal 4:19), but also and above all that of someone who is indebted to his predecessors, by whom he is welcomed in fellowship (Gal 2:9). Between Jesus and the apostolic activity of Paul there were about twenty years of developing ecclesial life in Jerusalem, Samaria, Damascus, and Syrian Antioch. It is in this period that faith in Jesus is consolidated ever more deeply in the minds and hearts of the first Christians and soon attains its original form, although subject to subsequent clarifications. Paul is indebted also to this development and to these churches. Consequently, having forcefully insisted on the fact that the call given directly to him by Christ was enough to authenticate his gospel, without having to await the approval of those who were apostles before him (Gal 1:11-17), he nevertheless feels an urgent need to connect the revelation he received with the common heritage by visiting Cephas (Gal 1:18) and comparing the content of his preaching with that of the others, "in order to make sure that I was not running, or had not run, in vain" (Gal 2:2). Likewise, although highlighting the primacy of his apostolic labors ("I worked harder than any of them," 1 Cor 15:10), Paul hastens to declare, "Whether then it was I or they, so we proclaim and so you have come to believe" (1 Cor 15:11).

He refuses, therefore, any form of local separatism which would cut one church off from the others and asks the Corinthians: "Did the word of God originate with you? Or are you the only ones it has reached?" (1 Cor 14:36). There are many divisions in this church: small groups which, also in a polemical way, side with various church figures (chaps. 1–4); celebrations of the Lord's Supper itself with "class" distinctions (1 Cor 11:17-34); rivalries for the most popular charisms (chaps. 12–14). A similar situation of division explains the broad sweep of Paul's opening greeting: "To the church of God that is in Corinth, to those who are sanctified in Christ Jesus, called to be saints, together with all those who in every place call on the name of our Lord Jesus Christ, both their Lord and ours" (1:2). This community, beset by so many threats of disintegration, is rightly exhorted by Paul to remember the many important components of unity: the undivided Christ (1:13); baptism in a single Spirit (12:13); the Eucharist (10:14-17; 11:23-34); love (8:1; 13; 16:24).

3.4.2 God Reveals Himself in the Crucified and Risen Christ

93. The death on the cross of the Son of God is the heart of the revealed truth proclaimed by Paul (1 Cor 2:1-2). It is "the message about the cross" (1 Cor 1:18), which is opposed to the pretensions of Jews and Greeks (1:22-23). To the boasting of the Greeks, proud of their "wisdom," he opposes the "foolishness" of the cross (1:23). Paul reacts also to the legalism of the Galatians: nothing can be added to Christ, not even the law which God gave as a preparatory element and which Christ brought to fulfillment—and surpassed.

It is really surprising that to counteract the self-sufficiency of the Corinthians, Paul does not have recourse to the resurrection, which would have counterbalanced very well the scandal of the cross. Even though the resurrection has a unique importance in his gospel (preaching and faith are vain without the resurrection; 1 Cor 15:14), Paul wished to counter the triumphalism of the Corinthians by reminding them that one does not arrive at Easter without first passing through Golgotha. We should note how he uses the perfect participle *estauroménos* (1:23; 2:2; Gal 3:1) when referring to the crucified One, thus indicating the extent to which Christ, though now glorified, continues to be the crucified One as well. It is evident, therefore, that God definitively manifests himself through the scandal of the cross of Christ, showing himself as a God of grace who prefers the weak, the sinners, and those far away. He is present and acts there where no one could possibly imagine: in Jesus of Nazareth, condemned to death on the cross.

But "death no longer has dominion over him" (Rom 6:9). Here we should note again that Paul never presents the resurrection as a fact independent of the cross. There is an absolute identity between the crucified and the risen One; there is, therefore, no discontinuity between the one who "humbled himself, becoming obedient even to death, death on a cross" and the one whom God "exalted" and to whom he "gave the name that is above every name," that is, the name "Lord" (*Kyrios*; Phil 2:8-9, 11). By simply looking at the crucified One, we would not notice any difference between Jesus and the other two criminals condemned with him, or between Jesus and the crucified hero Spartacus. On the other hand, if we were to consider only the risen One, we would end up with a religion that is abstract, alienating, and forgetful of the way (*of the cross*) that must be trodden before attaining glory. It was certainly the encounter with Christ, the conqueror of death, which led Paul to understand the vitality of the crucified One, and not vice versa. This was possible through both the personal experience of the apostles (Gal 1:15-16; 1 Cor 9:1; 15:8) and the mediation of the Church (1 Cor 11:23; 15:3: "I handed on to you . . . what I in turn had received").

3.4.3 Salvation Is Received and Lived within the Church, the Body of Christ

94. The fundamental and unique harmony between diversity and unity in the Christian communities led Paul to employ the metaphor of the "body" to meditate more deeply on the mysteries of the Church of Christ. This is a consideration which, in the New Testament, is exclusively Pauline (1 Cor 12:12-27; Rom 12:4-5). It is considerably developed in the letters to the Colossians (1:18, 22, 24; 2:9-19) and Ephesians (2:15-16; 4:4, 12-16; 5:28-33), which, according to many, belong to a later "Pauline school."

Speaking of Christians as the "Body of Christ," Paul goes beyond a simple comparison: the members of Christ constitute a single unit with him; the Church is a Body "in him." The Church is not the product of a sum of individuals and their collaboration, since it existed before the aggregation to it of each member. The result, therefore, is not something neutral (in Greek, *hen*) but something personal (*heis*): "There is no longer Jew or Greek, there is no longer slave or free, there is no longer male and female; for all of you are one [*heis*] in Christ Jesus" (Gal 3:28).

This passage teaches that "in the one Spirit we were all baptized into one body" (1 Cor 12:13). Almost as if pre-announcing the use of this metaphor, Paul had already underlined the original source of this unity: "Now there are varieties of gifts, but the same Spirit; and there are varieties of services, but the same Lord; and there are varieties of activities, but it is the same God who activates all of them in everyone" (1 Cor 12:4-6). He thus underlines the way such differences, harmonized in the Church's unity, reflect the original divine unity in which they are rooted. The same message is also contained in the precious concluding blessing in 2 Corinthians 13:13: "The grace of the Lord Jesus Christ, the love of God, and the communion of the Holy Spirit be with all of you." Paul's greeting begins not with God the Father but with Jesus Christ, because it was he alone who introduced us to the Trinitarian mystery (Rom 8:39). Finally, we should also note the task of the Holy Spirit to create communion, because it is his role to bring about the work of salvation throughout the ages, "In order that in Christ Jesus the blessing of Abraham might come to the Gentiles, so that we might receive the promise of the Spirit through faith" (Gal 3:14). Thus all have been given to drink of the one Spirit (1 Cor 12:13), and all form a fraternal community, diversified but of one mind. The priceless gift of this unity, which overcame even the ancient division between "Jew and Greek" (Rom 10:12; 1 Cor 1:24; 12:13; Gal 3:28), obliges us to walk "in newness of life" (Rom 6:4), in "the new life of the Spirit" (Rom 7:6), in such a way that "if anyone is in Christ, there is a new creation: everything old has passed away; see, everything has become new!" (2 Cor 5:17).

3.4.4 The Fullness of Salvation Consists
in the Resurrection of Christ

95. Union with Christ, which one lives together with other believers in the Body of Christ which is the Church, is not restricted to this earthly life; Paul even says: "If for this life only we have

hoped in Christ, we are of all people most to be pitied" (1 Cor 15:19). In the longest chapter of all his letters (1 Cor 15:1-58), he seeks to ground and explain the resurrection of Christians, which he derives from the resurrection of Christ. He strongly affirms that "Christ has been raised from the dead, the first fruits of those who have died . . . ; all will be made alive in Christ" (1 Cor 15:20, 22). Faith in the resurrection of Christ, in eternal communion with him and the Father, constitutes the foundation and the horizon of Paul's preaching. It has a profound influence on our life on earth and makes us capable of bearing difficulties and sufferings knowing that "in the Lord your labor is not in vain" (1 Cor 15:58). In his earliest letter, the apostle explains to the Thessalonians: "Through Jesus, God will bring with him those who have died" (1 Thess 4:14), and this, "so that you may not grieve as others do who have no hope" (1 Thess 4:13).

Paul does not give a description of such a life but simply asserts: "We will be with the Lord forever" (1 Thess 4:17; cf. 2 Cor 5:8). He recognizes in this faith and in this hope a great force for encouragement and consolation, and, at the end of the passage, he says to the Christians of Thessalonica: "Therefore encourage one another with these words" (1 Thess 4:18). Looking at his own death, Paul says: "My desire is to depart and be with Christ, for that is far better" (Phil 1:23). Being with Christ who is with the Father, which is the definitive and perfect communion of life with him and in him, and with all the members of his Body, is revealed as the fullness of salvation (cf. 1 Cor 15:28; also John 17:3, 24).

3.5 The Book of Revelation

3.5.1 Introduction: A Revealed, Unique, and Evocative Truth

96. The revealed truth contained in the message of Revelation is designated as "the revelation of Jesus Christ, which God gave him" (Rev 1:1). In the course of the book, this revealed truth, given by God the Father to Jesus Christ, is gradually explained as an initiative, a creative and salvific project, which, born in the intimacy of God, is then actualized outside of God on a human level. God

himself, Jesus Christ, and the inspired word of God are at work for the realization of the project. We can give a specific name to the object of this creative, salvific project: the Kingdom of God, which, conceived by God, embraces the entire created universe and develops within human history through Christ and Christians, until impelled and borne along by the word of Christ, it reaches its eschatological culmination in the splendor of the New Jerusalem (cf. Rev 21:1–22:5).

The development of the Kingdom of God in history proceeds in a dialectical way: there is a radical opposition which becomes a fierce struggle between the "structure of Christ," comprising Jesus Christ and his followers, and the "earthly structure" of evil, inspired and activated by the Demoniacal, which aims to establish its own anti-kingdom opposed to the Kingdom of God. The struggle will conclude, in the end, with the definitive disappearance of all the protagonists of evil and the full realization of the Kingdom of God in the definitive setting of "a new heaven and a new earth" (21:1), when a voice coming from the throne of the Kingdom of God will solemnly declare: "See, the home of God is among mortals. He will dwell with them; they will be his peoples, and God himself will be with them; he will wipe every tear from their eyes. Death will be no more; mourning and crying and pain will be no more, for the first things have passed away" (21:3-4). This is the most beautiful presentation of the realized Kingdom of God.

But the acute sense that the author of Revelation has of the actual human being in general, and specifically of the enormous difficulties the Christian encounters in the face of the hostile initiatives of the "earthly structure," lead him to underline the certainty of the full realization of the Kingdom of God. The Kingdom will be realized on earth, within the human realm, with all the fullness with which it was planned at the highest divine level.

We have, therefore, the Kingdom of God, viewed, on the one hand, in its overall global reality, and, on the other, accompanied and analyzed in its actual formation. These two aspects, when combined together, add up and present a fascinating and uniform picture of the Kingdom of God and of its becoming. This is the revealed truth typical of Revelation, which we can now see in detail.

3.5.2 Global Truth: The Kingdom of God as Realized by a Creative and Salvific Design

97. The first occurrences of the Kingdom found already at the beginning of the book offer us a revealing scenario: the liturgical assembly, turning to Jesus Christ crucified and risen, whom it feels to be present and close by, expresses its thanks for the gifts it receives from him with a surge of touching gratitude: "To him who loves us and freed us from our sins by his blood, and made us to be a kingdom, priests serving his God and Father, to him be glory and dominion forever and ever. Amen" (1:5-6). Reached by the love of Jesus Christ, Christians recognize that they are members of the Kingdom of God in Christ. It is a Kingdom that is in the process of developing and becoming, certainly not concluded, but already initiated: between the Christians and Jesus Christ there is a mutual belonging in love, one with a priestly responsibility for Christians which makes them mediators between God, Christ, and the human reality.

But even before this declaration from the liturgical assembly, we find a reference to the Kingdom in the opposite sense. Imparting the Trinitarian blessing to the assembly, John adds: "and from Jesus Christ, the faithful witness, the firstborn of the dead, and the ruler of the kings of the earth" (1:5). Along with the kingship of God and of Christ, there emerges an opposing kingship; in Revelation, the "kings of the earth" indicate centers of power characteristic of the "earthly system" opposed to the Kingdom of God (cf. 6:15; 17:2; 18:3, 9; 19:19). Between the Christians who already belong to the Kingdom of God and the anti-kingdom of evil, an opposition springs up that will bring them to share and to support, as his priests, the triumphant opposition of the Christ-Lamb (cf. 5:6-10).

The managing of the development of the Kingdom of God in history belongs to Christ-Lamb himself. Solemnly presented with the term "Lamb," a term that comes from the Fourth Gospel (cf. John 1:29, 36), John adds to the power to "take away the sin of the world" (cf. John 1:29) the energy that permits him to conquer and annihilate all the evil realized by the Demoniac and, positively, to share the Holy Spirit, of which he is the bearer, with all human beings who wish to belong to him (cf. Rev 5:6). To him the heavenly

Father solemnly entrusts the entire creative and salvific plan of the Kingdom (cf. Rev 5:7). And it will be he who will guide as his priestly mediators all those who are constituted as Kingdom. And the understanding of love, which united Jesus Christ and the Christians who adhere to him as his incipient kingdom, grows and develops as their collaboration proceeds.

The author of Revelation tends to underline most strongly this understanding of love, placing it, in his own characteristic style, within the human scheme of the love of two betrothed. Between Jesus Christ, then, and those who participate in his Kingdom, a reciprocity is established which has the freshness, the radicality, the overwhelming force, and the tenderness of a "first love" (cf. 2:4-5), a jealous love (3:19). And Jesus Christ demands this in a definite manner (cf. 2:4-5). It is evident that the Kingdom of God which he is called upon to build must be a Kingdom of love.

The feeling of reciprocal love between Jesus and his own develops in tandem with their collaboration in overcoming evil and in implanting good, tending toward its ultimate realization; when Christians reach this goal, their love for Jesus Christ will transform their engagement into marriage. Moving from the actual level of conflict between the "system of Christ" and the "earthly system" to the level of ultimate fulfillment, the author, with great joy, becomes aware of the full realization of the Kingdom of God and a heavenly voice which says to him: "Now have come the salvation and the power and the Kingdom of our God and the authority of his Messiah" (12:10). The book of Revelation, although acutely aware of the disturbing pressure of evil—and it will speak of it explicitly—insists on this positive conclusion of history. The thought of the Kingdom of God realized fascinates the writer and, in what is one of his most beautiful doxologies (cf. 19:1-9), he expresses himself in enthusiastic terms: "'Hallelujah! For the Lord our God the Almighty reigns. Let us rejoice and exult and give him the glory, for the marriage of the Lamb has come, and his bride has made herself ready; to her it has been granted to be clothed with fine linen, bright and pure'—for the fine linen is the righteous deeds of the saints" (19:6-8). With the "righteous deeds" of their collaboration with Christ, Christians are regarded as the fiancée who makes the bridal dress. The "wedding of the Lamb" will take place when, through the combined commitment of Jesus Christ and those who belong to him, all the evil in the world will have disappeared and all the operators of evil will have been destroyed, and the commitment of Jesus Christ and his own will have communicated the newness of Christ to all. And Christians, prepared by the touch of God, will be able to love Jesus Christ just as Jesus Christ loved and continues to love them. The "fiancée" will have become the "bride."

She is the marvel of the New Jerusalem, of the Kingdom of God by now brought to completion. No longer engaged in the unfolding of the Kingdom of God, Christians will be fully part of it and will enjoy it in its totality. The wonderful concluding page of the book tells us this (cf. 22:1-5). In the central square of the new Jerusalem there is a single throne, that "of God and the Lamb" (22:1c). From the throne streams "the river of the water of life, as clear as crystal" (22:1ab), symbol of the Holy Spirit. The river flows, giving birth to and developing "the tree of life" (22:2c), no longer as a single plant (cf. Rev 2:7; Gen 2:9; 3:22, 24), but as a forest of life "on either side of the river" (Rev 22:2b). Given the joint involvement of God the Father, Son, and Holy Spirit, we have, one could say, an endless "Trinitarian inundation" of life and of love, which reaches humanity. And human beings, joyful because they now form the kingdom in its fullness and are consequently able to love without limits, will no longer need the "light of lamp or sun, for the Lord God will be their light, and they will reign forever and ever" (22:5). See the great project of the Kingdom of God realized.

3.5.3 In-Depth Study of the "Veracity" That Leads to the Entire Truth

98. The great truth revealed in Revelation, concentrated in the Kingdom of God, is taken up again and studied in depth in the ten occurrences of the term "true." Related as they are to the revealed truth of the Kingdom of God, these occurrences illustrate and underline the extraordinarily coherent relationship that exists between the project seen from within God, in the divine intimacy, and its realization outside of God, in the reality of human history. And at

this point the hope of the Christian pilgrim takes off. Despite all the exasperating pressure of evil, the Kingdom "of our God and the authority of his Messiah" (12:10), far from being a transitory dream, will appear in their total reality.

a) The Truthfulness of God the Father

The first of the four attributions of the term "true" to God the Father relates to him personally. The martyrs, by now in direct contact with God, verifying the persistent presence of evil in the world, put a question to God that is crucial and charged with emotion, crying out with a loud voice: "Sovereign Lord, holy and *true*, how long will it be before you judge and avenge our blood on the inhabitants of the earth?" (6:10). The martyrs, beholding God directly, become aware of the absolute omnipotence that makes him "Sovereign Lord" of all; they see God as "the holy one" and, as such, radically opposed to evil, with the irresistible drive to eliminate it; they see God as "true," with an absolute coherence between all that he is in himself and his actions in history; distressed, they ask him how long his intervention will be delayed. God responds, reassuring them: his action to overcome evil will come about without fail, but it will gradually come about according to his plan. In the meantime, the martyrs immediately receive their direct participation in the resurrection of Christ, symbolized by the "white robe" (6:11) that was given them.

What we are seeing here is confirmed and explained when the term "true" refers to those effective elements with which God carries his project forward in history. These are the "ways" (cf. 15:3) and also some value "judgments" (cf. 16:7; 19:2) which, placing God in contact with human development, guarantee, insofar as they are "true," the utmost coherence between God in himself and all his activity.

b) The Truthfulness Proper to Christ

99. In the passage of the gift from Jesus Christ to humanity, characteristic of the project of the Kingdom of God, the term *true* is inserted three times (Rev 3:7, 14; 19:9), leading to a more complete understanding of the Kingdom itself and its becoming.

In the first of these occurrences, Jesus defines himself as "the holy one, the *true* one" (3:7), thereby placing himself on the same level as the Father to whom the martyrs had cried: "You who are holy and *true*" (6:10). Insofar as he is "holy," Jesus, like the Father, possesses the fullness of divinity. When the Father and Jesus enter into human history, the title "true" is applied to both, in the sense, seen above, of a perfect correspondence between their divinity and their involvement in history. Their contact with humanity, in the grand scheme of God, will not happen at a reduced level.

Looking at Jesus Christ engaged with human beings, another aspect of his presence in the reality of history emerges: it is the testimony of the Father, of which he is the bearer. As the "living Word," he sees the Father directly in his immensity; as the "incarnate Word," he stands in close contact with human beings, understanding them in every way. His testimony will thus be able to bring the infinite riches of the Father, whom he sees, within reach of human beings, as they are and where they are. Defining himself as "the faithful and *true* witness" (3:14), Jesus Christ underlines how his "faithful" testimony corresponds totally to the infinite riches of the Father and is at the same time in close contact with humankind. In addition, the qualification *true* makes clear how Jesus Christ commits in his testimony the fullness of his divinity and his humanity. The infinite riches of the Father, which are thus revealed to us in Jesus Christ, give body and substance to the revealed truth of the great project of the Kingdom. He reveals it and bestows it.

In the animated context which sees Christ and his own engaged, in the face of the earthly system, in uprooting evil and planting good, Christ "is called faithful and *true*" (19:11), which denotes his fidelity to the Father's project and the total commitment of his divinity and humanity to realize it. Some aspects of this truth are pointed out and underlined: he is compelled by a burning love ("his eyes are like a flame of fire"; 19:12) for the Father and for all human beings; he gives his life to fulfill his mission (he wears a "robe dipped in blood"; 19:13a); his name will remain unknown and at the outset will constitute his secret (19:12c). But when, through the word which he speaks (the "sharp sword" that comes out of his mouth; 19:15), he will have impressed on all those who receive him an imprint of himself, then his name will be recognized and he will be "called" publicly "the Word of God" (19:13b). This veritable and living "Word of God," which Jesus Christ bears within himself and with which he coincides perfectly as *logos* incarnate (cf. John 1:1, 14), conveyed by his word addressed to human beings, will be as though imprinted in all human beings who receive him and bestows on them his Christological newness. Everything, in the end, will be configured in him, gifted Word.

c) The Truth of the Inspired and Inspiring Words

100. In the first of the three occurrences of *true* that refer to the words (Rev 19:9), the interpreting angel who follows John speaks in these terms: "These words of God are *true*." The inspired words which we meet in Revelation are all basically words of God; they pass to and are concentrated in Jesus Christ, living Word of God; from Jesus Christ through his Spirit, they are radiated toward human beings and reach them. They are called "true" because they are capable of carrying and applying to the person who welcomes them all the riches of Christ and of God of which they are bearers.

The second occurrence has a more complicated literary formulation. Alternating here is a direct intervention of God, a resumption of the interpreting angel's discourse and, again, the concluding intervention of God: "And the one who was seated on the throne said, 'See, I am making all things new.' And [the interpreting angel] added: 'Write this, for these words are trustworthy and true.' And [God seated on the throne] said to me: 'It is done! I am the Alpha and the Omega, the beginning and the end'" (21:5-6). The solemn affirmation of God who, presented "seated on the throne," is seen as the determining source of the entire unfolding of revealed truth, of the full development of the Kingdom, shows the purpose that constantly moves him: he wishes to imprint in all things, beginning with humankind, the newness of Christ. The resumption of the interpreting angel's discourse addressed to John underlines its value and will be set down in writing: all "these words" of God (cf. 19:9), starting from those spoken last, "are faithful," corresponding adequately to the objective of God who destines them for humanity through Jesus Christ. Having, then, a dynamic content fully coherent with the demands of God and the aspirations of humankind, they are called "true," bearers, as they are, of the whole "newness" of Christ and capable of communicating it.

Having reached the eschatological goal, the words of God present in Revelation can be considered as "accomplished." The fact is solemnly affirmed by God, who is so close to human history as to coincide almost with its beginning and its completion. In the span of time between the "Alpha" and the "Omega," the "beginning" and the "completion," lie the "becoming" words of God; they develop dynamically and radiate their Christological content. And through these words which "come to be" God "makes all things new."

The third occurrence of "true" referring to the inspired words comes on the last page of the book. Once again, the interpreter angel declares to the liturgical assembly which is listening: "These words are trustworthy and *true*" (22:6). To the significance of a full correspondence with the objective of God and of a full commitment, always by God, to place his divinity at the service of humanity by means of Christ, there is added here the reference to the book which has just been read to the assembly. The inspired words, duly received, become inspirational in the one who welcomes them and implant the ever new and renewing Christ, of whom they are bearers.

And so the circle closes. Originating from God the Father, everything passes on to Jesus Christ, the living Word of the Father. Jesus Christ, the living Word, makes himself word, sent and donated: a word, which departs from himself as content, reaches humankind and implants in them his newness. From the Christological level, thus formed and developed in human beings, gradually establishing in them an ineffable unity with Jesus Christ, the living Word, we reach the heavenly Father.

IV. Conclusion

101. The reader of Sacred Scripture cannot but be impressed by the manner in which texts so different in their literary form and historical roots have been united in a single canon and manifest a concord of truth which finds its full expression in the person of Christ.

4.1 The Literary and Theological Pronouncements of the Old Testament

The study of various literary collections in the Old Testament revealed the extraordinary riches of the self-manifestation of God in history. The Scriptures attest that God wishes to enter into communication with humanity, taking on multiple forms of mediation.

- The work of creation itself is the reflection of the divine will to be a God "for humanity": God takes the initiative of manifesting himself in a creative act which the biblical account describes as "good" (Gen 1:31), although revealing that this act is immediately confronted with the question of evil (Gen 3:1-24).

- God reveals himself equally in the unique story of the Israelite people with multiple salvific interventions—liberation from Egyptian slavery (Exod 14), liberation from idolatry (Exod 20; Deut 5)—and with the gift of the law, which educates Israel to a life open to love of neighbor (Lev 19).

- The prophetic literature qualifies the words of the prophets as inspired (in the introduction to the books, the messenger formula, and the oracle formulae). The prophetic oracles express both the demands of God revealed to the people in the midst of the vicissitudes of history and the fidelity of the Lord despite the faults of Israel.

- Wisdom literature, for its part, reflects the conflicts that can arise between the ancient cultures which aspire to the truth and the specific revelation of which Israel was the beneficiary. Common to the various wisdom traditions is the presentation of Israel's wisdom as the ultimate expression of divine truth. In particular, during the Hellenistic era, the wisdom of Israel, confronted with Greek philosophical systems, sought to propose a coherent system of thought which underlines the moral and theological significance of the Torah and which seeks to arouse the adherence of the heart and mind.

- The hymnic literature, especially the Psalms, integrates the whole spectrum of features mentioned previously: the Psalter celebrates God, Creator and Savior, God present in history,

God the source of life, at the same time inviting believers to live a faithful, just, and upright life.

4.2 The Theological Pronouncements of the New Testament

102. The project which brings the books of the New Testament together is that of bringing the reader to encounter the Christ, "revealer of the Father," source of salvation and ultimate manifestation of the truth. This common perspective assumes different pedagogical forms.

- The Synoptic Gospels, whose redactors base their accounts on direct historical testimony, demonstrate how Jesus of Nazareth "fulfilled" all the expectations of Israel: he is the Messiah, the Son of God, the mediator of salvation. Consecrated by the Spirit, he inaugurates, with his death and resurrection, a new time, the Kingdom of God.

- The Gospel according to John shows that Christ is the fullness of the Word of God, the Word revealed to his disciples, who receive the promise of the gift of the Spirit.

- The letters of Paul claim the authority of an apostle, who, beginning from his personal experience of Christ, spreads the Gospel among the pagans and, with a new vocabulary, proposes the work of Christ to the cultures of his time.

- According to Revelation, Jesus, who receives and gives the inspired word (cf. Rev 1:1), constitutes the supreme gift of the Father. An absolute correspondence exists between the plan of the Kingdom that God desires and its true actualization through Christ in human history. When the inspired words are all realized, destroying the evil embedded in history and implanting there the splendor of Christ, God will solemnly restate: "It is done" (Rev 21:6).

4.3 The Need for and the Methods of a Canonical Approach to Scripture

103. The Dogmatic Constitution *Dei Verbum* (n. 12) and the Post-Synodal Exhortation *Verbum Domini* (nn. 40–41) indicate

how only an approach which takes account of the entire canon of Scripture is adequate to unveil its full theological and spiritual sense. Every biblical tradition, in fact, must be interpreted in the canonical context in which it was articulated, which permits one to explain the diachronic and synchronic connections with the entire canon. The canonical approach thus points out the relationships between the traditions of the Old Testament and those of the New Testament.

Beyond the diversity described in the preceding paragraphs, the canon of Scripture refers, in fact, to a single Truth, the Christ, whom the apostolic testimony recognizes as Son of God, revealer of the Father, and the Savior of humanity. The entire canon culminates in this affirmation, toward which all the elements which comprise the canon "tend," so to speak. In other words, the canon of Scripture is the adequate interpretive context for each of the traditions of which it is composed: having been integrated into the canon, each particular tradition receives a new context of enunciation which renews its meaning.

This "canonical logic" takes account of the relationships that exist between the New and Old Testaments: the New Testament traditions employ the vocabulary of "necessity" and that of "fulfillment" (or "perfecting") in order to express how the life and work of Christ refer to the traditions of the Old Testament (cf. Matt 26:54; Luke 22:37; 24:44). The message of the Scriptures, to be truthful, *must necessarily be fulfilled*, and this fulfillment is fully realized in the life, death, and resurrection of Christ (John 13:18; 19:24; Acts 1:16). The very person of Christ confers the definitive meaning on very different traditions: we see him, for example, in chapter 24 of the Gospel of Luke, in which Jesus in person shows how his own individual story sheds light on the traditions of the Torah, the prophets, and the Psalms. The person of Christ responds thus to the expectations of Israel and brings the revelation of God to completion. The Christ "recapitulates" the principal figures of the first Covenant and links them together. He is the servant, the Messiah, the mediator of the new Covenant, the Savior.

On the other hand, the Christ expresses, in a final, unsurpassable way, the truth which has been revealed and progressively expressed in written traditions within the context of the first Covenant. The truth of Christ is handed on in the New Testament traditions, which provide an inseparable link between the eyewitness testimony of the first disciples and the reception, in the Spirit, of this testimony of the first Christian communities.

But this truth of God and the salvation of the human race, which constitutes the center of divine revelation and reaches its ultimate and definitive expression in Jesus, in what does it consist? We find the answer to this question in the activity of Jesus. He reveals God who is Father, Son, and Holy Spirit (Matt 28:19), the God who is and lives in himself perfect communion. Jesus calls his disciples to a communion of life with himself as they follow him (Matt 4:18-22) and commissions them to make all the people of all nations his disciples (Matt 28:19). He then expresses his greatest desire, asking the Father: "May they be with me where I am, to see my glory" (John 17:24). This is the truth revealed by and in Jesus: God is communion in himself, and God offers communion with himself through his Son (cf. *DV*, n. 2). Inspiration, whose Trinitarian character we recognized in the authors of the New Testament, appears as the proper way for the communication of this truth. There is a correspondence between inspiration and the truth of the Bible.

The canon of Scripture, therefore, gives access, at the same time, to the dynamic by which God communicates himself to human beings through the prophets, biblical writers, and finally in Jesus of Nazareth and also to the process by which the community receives this revelation in the Spirit and delivers its content in writing.

Part Three

The Interpretation of the Word of God and Its Challenges

I. Introduction

104. When introducing the preceding section, which dealt with the testimony of biblical writings about truth, we explained how *Dei Verbum* understands the truth of the Bible, commenting in particular on the phrase "the truth which God wanted put into the sacred writings for the sake of our salvation" (n. 11). We learned that the truth which the Bible wishes to communicate to us regards God himself and his plan of salvation for human beings.

We now look again at the truth of Sacred Scripture, but from a different point of view. In the Bible, we encounter contradictions, historical inaccuracies, implausible narratives, and, in the Old Testament, moral precepts and behavior in conflict with the teachings of Jesus. What is the "truth" of these biblical passages? Without doubt, we are faced with real challenges for the interpretation of the Word of God.

Indications of an answer to this question are offered in *Dei Verbum* itself. The conciliar text affirms that the revelation of God in salvation history takes place through events and words which complement each other (n. 2), but it also states that "imperfect and temporary things" (n. 15) are found in the Old Testament. It makes its own the teaching of the "*condescension* of eternal Wisdom" which comes from John Chrysostom (n. 13), but above all it appeals to "literary genres" employed in antiquity, referring to the encyclical *Divino Afflante Spiritu* of Pius XII (*EB* 557–62). It is this latter aspect that we need to examine in greater depth. Even today, the truth contained in a novel is different from that of a physics manual. There are different ways of writing history, which is not always an objective chronicle; lyric poetry does not express what is found in an epic poem, and so forth. This is valid also for the literature of the ancient Near East and the Hellenistic world. In the Bible, we find different literary genres in use in that cultural area: poetry, prophecy, narrative, eschatological sayings, parables, hymns, confessions of faith, etc., each of which has its own way of presenting the truth.

The narrative of Genesis 1–11, the traditions dealing with the patriarchs and the conquest of the land of Israel, the stories of the kings down to the Maccabean revolt certainly contain truths, but they do not intend to propose a historical chronicle of the people of Israel. The protagonist in salvation history is neither Israel nor other peoples but God. The biblical accounts are theologized narratives. Their truth—illustrated by some texts in the preceding section—is obtained from the recounted facts, but above all from the didactic, paraenetic, and theological purpose pursued by the author, who gathered these ancient traditions or worked on the material in the archives of the scribes, thus transmitting a prophetic or wisdom concept and communicating to his generation a decisive message.

105. On the other hand, a "history of salvation" does not exist without a historical nucleus, if it is true that God reveals himself by means of "deeds and words having an inner unity" (*DV*, n. 2). Moreover, if inspiration encompasses the Old and New Testaments in their entirety, "with all of their parts" (n. 11), we cannot eliminate any passage from the narrative; the exegete must strive to find the significance of every phrase in the context of the narrative as a whole by means of the various methods listed in the Pontifical Biblical Commission's document *The Interpretation of the Bible in the Church* (cf. *EB* 1259–60).

Although a diachronic study of the texts is indispensable to understand the different reinterpretations of an oracle or an original narrative, the true sense of a passage is its final form, accepted into the canon of the Church. The reinterpretation can also take the form of an allegorization of older texts. So, even if we take into consideration the imperfection of revelation in the Old Testament, certain narratives or psalms which speak of extermination and hate toward one's enemies, far from the spirit of the New Testament, can possess a paraenetic value for the generation to which they are addressed.

It is obvious that these considerations do not resolve all the difficulties, but it is undeniable that *Dei Verbum*, with the expression "the truth . . . for the sake of our salvation" (n. 11), restricts biblical truth to divine revelation which concerns God himself and the salvation of the human race. Moreover, the emphasis on literary genres has given broader scope to the work of exegetes, already difficult in itself. The following examples will illustrate this point.

II. First Challenge: Historical Problems

106. Here we are concerned with only a few problematic texts, some drawn from the Old Testament, others from the New. The passages are diverse in nature, but for all of them, even though in different forms and for specific reasons, we can ask the question: of that which is narrated, what actually happened? In what measure are the texts able and willing to attest facts that actually took place? What do they wish to affirm? The particular problematic of each passage will be indicated in the relevant paragraph.

2.1 The Abraham Cycle (Genesis)

The majority of exegetes concede that the final redaction of the patriarchal narratives, of those of Exodus, of the conquest, and of the Judges, was carried out during the Persian Period after the Babylonian Exile. With regard to the cycle of Abraham, the episodes which link the history of this patriarch to the other patriarchal traditions, in particular through accounts of promises, are more recent and go beyond a prospect originally limited to clan narratives. An episode like that of Genesis 15—essential for the thesis of Paul on justification by faith alone independent of works of the Mosaic law (cf. Rom 4)—does not describe the events in the precise way in which they took place, as its redactional history shows. But if this is the case, what can be said of the patriarch's act of faith and of Paul's argument, which seems to lose the scriptural support it needed?

The first thing that can be said about the patriarchal narratives (and also those of the Exodus and the conquest) is that they do not emerge out of thin air. All peoples, in fact, need to know and express, both for themselves and for others, where they come from, their geographical and temporal provenance, in other words, their origins. Like the surrounding peoples, the Israelites of the fifth and fourth centuries before Christ began to recount their past. Their accounts recalled ancient traditions, not only to affirm that they had a respectable history, like the other peoples, but also to interpret it and to evaluate it with the help of their faith.

107. What, then, was known about Abraham and the forefathers? Probably that they were shepherds coming from Mesopotamia, nomads who moved from one pasture to another, according to the seasons, the rains, and the welcome they received in the lands they were crossing. The post-exilic writers, whose reflection was nurtured by the memory of deportation and its importance for the faith of their community, understood that the generation of the Exile had experienced something similar to the experience of the patriarchs: they, in fact, had lost their land, their political and religious (the temple) institutions, and were forced to go into a strange land and live there as slaves. It was a dramatic situation which obliged them to live on faith and hope. Having lost that which constituted their identity as a people (that is, the land and their native institutions), the exiles should have disappeared—and yet they survived as a people thanks to their faith. This radical experience nourished their prayer and their rereading of the past. Without doubt, when the biblical narrator or narrators describe the divine promises and the patriarch Abraham's response of faith (Gen 15:1-6), they do not refer to facts whose secular transmission would have been absolutely secure. It was, rather, their experience of faith which allowed them to write in the way they did, to present the global significance of those events, and to invite their compatriots to believe in the power and faithfulness of God, who permitted them and their ancestors to pass through often dramatic historical periods. The interpretation of the

concrete facts, the sense which emerges from their interpretation in the "today" of the rereading, counts more than the facts themselves. Indeed, it is only with time that the meaning of a historical period which lasted for centuries can be understood and written down in the form of a theological account or a hymnic poem. With their living faith in God, the biblical writers meditated on the survival of their people through the centuries, despite the many mortal dangers and the terrible catastrophes they had to face; they also reflected on the role which God and their faith in him had played in such a survival; from this, they were able to conclude that it was like this also at the beginning of their history. Genesis 15, therefore, cannot be read as if it were a chronicle but rather as normative behavior willed by God, a standard which the biblical authors lived radically and which they were able to transmit to their generation and to future generations.

In short, to evaluate the truth of ancient biblical accounts, it is necessary to read them as they were written and as they were read by Paul himself: "These things happened to them to serve as an example, and they were written down to instruct us, on whom the ends of the ages have come" (1 Cor 10:11).

2.2 The Crossing of the Red Sea (Exod 14)

108. The account of the passage of the Israelites through the sea constitutes an essential part of the prescribed readings for the Christian celebration of the Easter Vigil. This account is based on a very ancient tradition which commemorates the liberation of a people who had been reduced to slavery. This oral tradition, put down in writing, was the object of multiple "rereadings" and, in the end, was inserted into the narrative of the Exodus and into the Torah. In this framework, the liberation of Israel is presented as a *new creation*. Just as God created the world by separating the sea and the dry land, in the same way he "created" the people of Israel, tracing out for them a passage on the dry land through the sea. The account, therefore, closely connects an ancient narrative tradition with a theological interpretation based on the theology of creation.

The truth of the account does not reside, therefore, solely in the tradition which it commemorates—an account of liberation which retains all its relevance during the Babylonian Exile, when subjugated Israel aspires to freedom—but also in the theological interpretation which accompanies it. The biblical text, therefore, combines in inseparable fashion, an *ancient account*, transmitted from generation to generation, with an *actualization* called for later. This actualization echoes the situation of the authors of Exodus 14 when the text was composed. In fact, alongside the theology of creation, the account develops a theology of salvation, presenting the God of Israel as the Savior who liberates his people from oppression and Moses as a prophetic figure who invites the people to have confidence in the saving power of its God: "Do not be afraid! Be strong, and you will see the salvation of the Lord!" (Exod 14:13). Just as in ancient times the Lord knew how to protect his people, in the same way, in every situation, he is capable of guarding them and procuring their salvation. The Exodus account does not intend primarily to transmit a record of ancient events in the manner of an archival document but rather to call to mind a tradition which attests that today, as yesterday, God is present along with his people to save them.

This experience and this hope of salvation, expressed in the account of Exodus 14, also have a liturgical tradition in the Passover account which precedes it (Exod 12:1–13:16). The Christian liturgy of the Easter Vigil shows how the account of Exodus 14 finds its "fulfillment" in Jesus Christ, through whose resurrection God the Creator and Savior manifested himself to his people in a definitive manner, beyond which one cannot go.

2.3 The Books of Tobit and Jonah

109. The book of Tobit does not belong to the Hebrew Bible but forms part of the Greek; the Council of Trent's decree on the canon includes it among the historical books of the Old Testament (*D-S* 1502). The book of Jonah, on the other hand, is to be found among the Twelve Prophets (also called the "Minor Prophets") in the Hebrew Bible. Both books recount a series of events which raise the question as to whether these events happened in reality.

2.3.1 The Book of Tobit

The death of the seven husbands of the same woman before the consummation of the marriage (3:8-17) is a fact so unlikely that, this, by itself, suggests that the narrative is a literary fiction. This also accounts for the numerous anachronisms: the father of the protagonist is presented as one of the Israelites deported to Nineveh and, at the same time, as one who observes the Deuteronomistic law (1:1-22); Tobiah "prophesies" also the destruction of Nineveh, the desolation of Judea and Samaria, the burning of the temple and its reconstruction (14:4-5).

We have here, then, a popular religious fable with a didactic and edifying purpose which, by its nature, places it in the sphere of the wisdom tradition. It is a literary composition with the well-known scheme—duplicated because of the parallelism between Tobiah and Sarah—of the conduct of the just man who, afflicted by tribulation, prays to the Lord who sends salvation.

The intervention of the demon Asmodeus derives from the biblical tradition which sees Satan and his angels active in our world and causing disasters. This permits us to classify the work within the literary genre of stories which have among their characters human and superhuman protagonists. In the book of Tobit, the intervention of the demon is presented very soberly, as distinct from many other narratives of this same genre. The demon Asmodeus is a fictitious character, but the diabolical capacity to harm human beings is not, especially if they are striving to live faithful to God. Consequently, the angel Raphael is also a character of literary fiction; however, in accordance with repeated and persistent biblical traditions and their reception by the Church, the ability of beings like him to intervene in aid of those who invoke the name of the Lord is not fictitious.

The book of Tobit is a manifesto in praise of the traditional pious practices of Judaism, prayer, fasting, and almsgiving (12:8-9), as well as the practice of works of mercy, in particular, burying the dead (12:13), and the prayer of blessing and thanksgiving which proclaims the glorious works of God (12:6, 22; 13:1-18). A particular aspect of the book is its insistence on the prayer which sanctifies conjugal life and which sustains one in times of danger (8:4-9).

2.3.2 The Book of Jonah

110. The fact that the book of Jonah was transmitted among the writings of the Twelve Prophets is an indication that its protagonist was regarded very early on as an authentic prophet (cf. 2 Kgs 14:25), to be placed historically in the context of the Assyrian Empire which the narrative presupposes, before the Babylonians and Medes began the destruction of Nineveh in 612 BC. Such an opinion seems supported by the fact that Jesus himself refers to the best-known episode in the story regarding the prophet, the three days and three nights spent in the belly of the whale, as a "historical" sign prefiguring the event of his own resurrection (Matt 12:39-41; Luke 11:29-30; Matt 16:4).

In the account, however, there are not only details but also structural elements which we cannot consider as historical events and which lead us to interpret the text as an imaginary composition with deep theological content.

A few improbable details—as, for example, that Nineveh was an extremely large city, a three-day journey across (Jonah 3:3)—may be considered hyperbole; among the structural elements, however, some are implausible—the fish which swallows Jonah and keeps him alive in its belly for three days and three nights before vomiting him up (2:1, 11) and the supposed conversion of the entire city of Nineveh (3:5-10), of which there is no trace anyway in Assyrian records.

Among the theological themes present in the narrative, we underline two: (a) the content of a prophetic message is not an irrevocable decree (3:4) but rather a pronouncement which is modified in light of the response of those to whom it is addressed (4:2, 11); (b) post-exilic Judaism was characterized by a tension between more conciliatory and universal tendencies and tendencies which were narrower and more exclusive. This appears clearly in the contrast between the books of Ruth, Jonah, and Tobit, on the one hand, and the books of Haggai, Zechariah, Ezra, Nehemiah, and Chronicles, on the other. Ezra and Nehemiah had made possible the maintaining of Jewish identity, opposing any mixing whatsoever with paganism, especially that represented by mixed marriages (Ezra 9–10; Neh 10:29-31). However, a more open and universal spirit, free to make use also of the ancient patriarchal and prophetic traditions, was never entirely lost. The book of Ruth reacts against the prohibition of mixed marriages, presenting a stranger, Ruth the Moabite (Ruth 1:4-19), as an antecedent of David (Ruth 4:17). Jonah goes further in its universalism, making the wicked and hated Assyrians—who destroyed the Kingdom of Israel, deported its inhabitants, and proudly boasted of its ferocious wartime tactics—the recipients of a prophetic message which rendered them capable of conversion.

2.4 The Gospel Infancy Narratives

111. Only Matthew (1–2) and Luke (1:5–2:52) placed at the head of their gospels a so-called infancy narrative in which the origin and beginnings of Jesus' life are set forth. There are striking differences between the two accounts and also the presence of extraordinary events which provoke wonder, such as the virginal conception of Jesus; the question of the historicity of such narratives thus arises. We will present the differences and agreements found in the two accounts and seek to determine the message offered by the two texts.

2.4.1 The Differences

Matthew places at the beginning a genealogy (1:1-17), noticeably different from that found in Luke 3:23-38, which is placed after the baptism of Jesus. The announcement of Jesus' conception by the Holy Spirit is made to Joseph (Matt 1:18-25). Jesus—born in Bethlehem of Judea (2:1), the land of Joseph and Mary—is visited and adored by angels and magi, who are guided by a star, unaware of the mortal threat posed by King Herod (2:1-11). Alerted in a dream, they return to their land by another route (2:12). Forewarned by an angel of the Lord in a dream, Joseph flees to Egypt with the child and its mother (2:13-15) before the slaughter of the infants in Bethlehem (2:16-18). After the death of Herod, Joseph, Mary, and the child return to their land and settle in Nazareth, where Jesus grows up (2:19-23).

In the account of Luke 1:5–2:52 the presence of John the Baptist and the parallel narratives on John and Jesus constitute elements of diversity. These relate to the annunciation of their births (1:5-25,

26-38), the births themselves, the circumcision of the children and the conferral of names (1:57-79; 2:1-21). Mary and Joseph live in Nazareth (1:26) and go to Bethlehem on account of the census of Quirinius (2:1-5). Jesus is born there (2:6-7) and is visited by shepherds, to whom an angel of the Lord announces his birth (2:8-20). The child is presented to the Lord in the Jerusalem temple, according to the prescriptions of the law, and is welcomed by Simeon and Anna (2:22-40). At twelve years of age, Jesus returns again to the temple (2:41-52).

Not one of the stories found in Matthew is present in Luke, and vice versa. There are other noteworthy differences between the two narratives. According to Matthew, Mary and Joseph live in Bethlehem before the birth of Jesus, and it is only after the flight into Egypt and following a particular warning that they go to Nazareth. According to Luke, Mary and Joseph live in Nazareth, the census brings them to Bethlehem, and they return to Nazareth without a flight into Egypt. It is difficult to find a solution for such differences. On the other hand, they reveal a reciprocal independence on the part of the two evangelists; this makes their agreements all the more significant.

2.4.2 The Agreements

112. Matthew and Luke both report the following particulars. Mary, the mother of Jesus, is betrothed to Joseph (Matt 1:18; Luke 1:27), who is of the house of David (Matt 1:20; Luke 1:27). The two do not live together before the conception of Jesus, which is brought about by the Holy Spirit (Matt 1:18, 20; Luke 1:35). Joseph is not the natural father of Jesus (Matt 1:16, 18, 25; Luke 1:34). The name of Jesus, together with its salvific meaning (Matt 1:21; Luke 2:11), is communicated by an angel (Matt 1:21; Luke 1:31). Jesus is born in Bethlehem at the time of King Herod (Matt 2:1; Luke 2:4-7; 1:5) and grows up in Nazareth (Matt 2:22-23; Luke 2:39, 51). The basic data regarding persons, places, and time are common to the two evangelists. Of particular importance is their agreement concerning the virginal conception of Jesus by the Holy Spirit, which excludes the possibility that Joseph is the natural father of Jesus.

2.4.3 The Message

113. The infancy narratives of Matthew and Luke introduce the rest of their work and show how what is manifested in the life and ministry of Jesus is based on his origins. Through the different accounts and titles conferred on Jesus, these infancy narratives explain the relationship of Jesus with God, his mission as Savior, his universal role, his painful destiny, and his place in God's dealings with the people of Israel.

Matthew presents Jesus as the Son of God (2:15) in whom God is present and to whom the name "Emmanuel," "God is with us," belongs (1:23). God imposes the name "Jesus," in which the program of his salvific mission is expressed: "He will save his people from their sins" (1:21). Jesus is the Christ of the house of David (1:1, 16, 17, 18; 2:4) "who will shepherd my people Israel" (2:6; cf. Mic 5:1), the last and definitive king God gives to his people. The arrival of the Magi shows that the mission of Jesus goes beyond Israel and involves all nations (Matt 2:1-12). The deadly threat, which comes from the king of that time (2:1-18) and continues with his successor (2:22), foreshadows the passion and death of Jesus. The fact that Jesus is rooted in the people of Israel is present throughout the whole account and is concentrated in the genealogy (1:1-17) and in the four fulfillment citations (1:22-23; 2:15, 17-18, 23; cf. 2:6).

Similar indications are to be found in Luke, even though the expression and emphases are different. Jesus is called "Son of God" (1:35; cf. 1:32), and his first words, the only ones recorded from the gospel infancy narratives, are spoken in the temple: "I must be in my Father's house" (2:49). In announcing his birth to the shepherds, the angel proclaims that "a Savior, who is the Messiah, the Lord" (2:11), is born. In "the Lord's Messiah" (2:26), "salvation" (2:30) and the "redemption of Jerusalem" (2:38) have arrived. The link between Jesus and David is underlined (1:26, 69; 2:4, 11), culminating in the announcement of the angel: "The Lord God will give to him the throne of his ancestor David. He will reign over the house of Jacob forever, and of his kingdom there will be no end" (1:32-33). The universal significance of Jesus' coming is expressed by Simeon: the salvation which comes about in Jesus is "in the presence of all peoples" (2:31), and Jesus is "a light for revelation to the Gentiles"

(2:32). Simeon also makes reference to the difficulties of Jesus' mission, speaking of the "sign that will be opposed" (2:34). What is recounted in Luke's infancy narrative is situated in the religious life of Israel: it begins with a sacrifice in the temple (1:5-22) and finishes with a pilgrimage to the temple (2:41-50) in faithful observance of the law of the Lord (2:21-28).

114. Both evangelists refer to the virginal conception of Jesus by the Holy Spirit and attribute the beginning of Jesus' life exclusively to the action of God, without the intervention of a human father. In Matthew 1:20-23, the announcement of the birth of Jesus is linked to his salvific mission: the one who will save his people from their sins and will reconcile them with God, the one who is "God with us," has a divine origin. Both the Savior and salvation come from God alone; they are gifts of his grace. In Luke 1:35 the consequence of Jesus' virginal conception is indicated: "Therefore the child to be born will be holy; he will be called Son of God." Jesus' relationship to God is manifested in his virginal conception. Insofar as he is "holy," he belongs totally to God, and in his human life too, God alone is his Father. The virginal conception of Jesus has a profound significance both for his relationship with God and for his salvific mission on behalf of all human beings.

In light of the differences and the agreements which we find in the infancy narratives of the two evangelists, it must be said that salvific revelation consists in all that is said about the person of Jesus and about his relationship with the history of Israel and the world as an introduction to and an illustration of his saving work recounted in the rest of the gospel. The differences, which can be harmonized in part, refer to secondary aspects common to the two evangelists that relate to the central figure of Jesus, the Son of God and Savior of humanity.

2.5 The Miracle Narratives

115. In the Old and New Testaments, extraordinary events are narrated which do not correspond to what normally happens; they go beyond what human beings are capable of and are attributed to a special intervention of God. For a long time, by reason of a

scientific approach, simply taken for granted, and because of certain philosophical concepts, doubts arose as to the historicity of these stories. According to modern science, everything that happens in this world happens on the basis of invariable rules: the so-called laws of nature. Everything is determined by these laws, and there is no space for extraordinary happenings. There is also a widespread philosophical concept according to which God, although Creator of the world, does not intervene in its functioning, which runs according to fixed rules. In other words, it is asserted that there cannot be extraordinary events caused by God; the narratives which speak of these events, therefore, cannot have any historical truth.

Let us now consider the miracle accounts present in the Old and New Testaments, seeking their meaning within their literary contexts. The New Testament accounts are in continuity with the traditions of the people of Israel and reveal that the creative and salvific power of God reaches its fullness in Jesus Christ.

2.5.1 Narratives in the Old Testament

116. The books of the Old Testament are pervaded by the belief that God has created everything, works continually in the world, and holds all things in existence and in life. With its faith, the people of Israel see the created world with all its wonders as the effect of the direct action of God, whether they be ordinary or extraordinary events; everything is one continuous great miracle. Everything is a message of faith, which is well summed up with these words of the psalm: "[He] alone does great wonders, for his steadfast love endures forever" (Ps 136:4).

This faith is expressed in the form of a hymn, characterized by gratitude, joy, and praise, in texts such as Psalm 104 and Sirach 43 (cf. Gen 1). Psalm 104, which is dedicated to God the Creator, is followed by Psalm 105, in which the power and fidelity of God in the history of his people Israel are celebrated. God, who created all things and is at work in creation, is also at work in history (cf. Pss 106; 135; 136). His action is revealed in a particularly wonderful and extraordinary way in the liberation of Israel from slavery in Egypt and in guiding Israel to the promised land. Moses, commissioned and empowered by God, performs miraculous actions of which the book of Exodus and many other texts speak (among which also Ps 105:26-45). One may note the great influence which the progressive liberation of Israel had on the traditions up to their rereading in Wisdom 15:14–19:17. But it does not seem possible to ascertain with certainty what actually happened. Through these traditions, people remember, express themselves, and recognize that God acts in history and that he guided and saved his people with power and fidelity.

2.5.2 The Miracles of Jesus

117. All four gospels present a series of extraordinary actions performed by Jesus. The most frequent of these are the healings of sick people and the exorcisms. Also recounted are three raisings of dead persons (Matt 9:18-26; Luke 7:11-17; John 11:1-44) and several "miracles of nature": the calming of the storm (Matt 8:23-27), Jesus walking on the water (Matt 14:22-33), the multiplication of the loaves and fish (Matt 14:13-21 and parallels), and the changing of water into wine (John 2:1-11). Like the teaching in parables, the performing of extraordinary actions by Jesus is also part of his ministry and is attested in many ways. These accounts do not constitute a later addition to the original traditions about the ministry of Jesus.

The terms with which the evangelists describe these actions are significant. Although they tell of the amazement of the crowds at the actions of Jesus (cf. Matt 9:33; Luke 9:43; 19:17; John 7:21), the gospels do not use a term that corresponds to our term "miracle" (which signifies "a work which provokes amazement"). The Synoptic Gospels speak of "works of power" (*dynameis*), while John's gospel uses the term "signs" (*semeia*). This difference in terminology is very significant. In all the extraordinary actions performed by Jesus, the overcoming of some situation of need (illness, danger, etc.) takes place immediately. Afterward, with his behavior, Jesus points out that this extraordinary happening does not end here. Matthew 11:20 reads: "Then he began to reproach the cities in which most of his deeds of power had been done, because they did not repent" (cf. Luke 10:13). It is not enough to admire and to thank the wonder-worker: conversion must follow his message. In the Synoptic Gospels, the Kingdom of God is at the heart of Jesus' proclamation (cf. Matt 4:17; Mark 1:15; Luke 4:43). The mighty deeds must confirm and make clear that the salvific reality of this Kingdom has drawn near and become present. With regard to his activity, Jesus says: "But if it is by the Spirit of God that I cast out demons, then the kingdom of God has come to you" (Matt 12:28; cf. Luke 11:20). These deeds, in their diversity, not only manifest the different aspects of the salvific power of the Kingdom of God but also serve the purpose of revealing the identity of Jesus. After he had calmed the stormy sea, the disciples ask themselves: "What sort of man is this, that even the winds and the sea obey him?" (Matt 8:27). The question of John the Baptist, "Are you the one who is to come?" is prompted "by the works of the Messiah" (Matt 11:2-3). Jesus responds to his question by listing his mighty deeds (11:4-5).

In the Gospel of John, the extraordinary deeds of Jesus are called "signs": these, therefore, propose a different reality. With regard to the first extraordinary deed, the transformation of water into wine at Cana, the Evangelist says: "Jesus did this, the first of his signs, in Cana of Galilee, and revealed his glory; and his disciples believed in him" (John 2:11). The revelation of Jesus' glory, that is, his relationship with God and his "glory as of a Father's only Son" (John 1:14), leading to faith in Jesus, is the real meaning and purpose of the signs. Frequently linked to the signs is an instruction of Jesus which indicates a specific aspect of its salvific meaning. In the multiplication of the loaves (6:1-58), Jesus reveals himself as "the bread of life" (6:35, 48, 51); in the healing of the blind man (9:1-41), as "the light of the world" (9:5; cf. 8:12; 12:46); in the raising of Lazarus (11:1-44), as "the resurrection and the life" (11:25). In the first ending of his gospel, John highlights the signs of Jesus and speaks directly to his readers: "But these [signs] are written so that you may come to believe that Jesus is the Messiah, the Son of God, and that through believing you may have life in his name" (20:31). The disciples (20:30) are the eyewitnesses, and everyone else depends on their testimony. The signs attested and written down have the purpose of leading to faith in Jesus, not a vague faith, but one that is clearly spelled out and leads, therefore, to that life which comes from him.

John also frequently uses the term "works" (*erga*) to define the extraordinary actions of Jesus. After the healing of a sick man on the Sabbath day (5:1-18), Jesus explains (5:19-47) how his activity depends on that of the Father: "The works that the Father has given me to complete, the very works that I am doing, testify on my behalf that the Father has sent me" (5:36; cf. 10:25, 37-38; 12:37-43). The term "works" underlines another characteristic of Jesus' actions: they are "signs" for human beings and are "works" which correspond to the activity of God the Father. For this reason, they testify to the fact that Jesus was sent by God the Father.

118. Finally, mention should be made of the goal and culmination of all the signs and works of Jesus: his resurrection. This is no longer a visible sign and is the work of God the Father, for "God raised him from the dead" (Rom 10:9; cf. Gal 1:1; etc.). The resurrection of Jesus was not seen by anyone but was made known to the disciples, who become its witnesses (cf. Acts 10:41), through the appearances of the risen Christ. The aim of the signs and of the works accomplished by Jesus was to reveal his relationship with God and to show his salvific mission, a mission which is expressed as alleviation of human misery and communication of life. All this is now brought to completion by his resurrection. This reveals and confirms the closest union between God and Jesus, it signifies the overcoming of death and of all infirmities, and it achieves the passage to perfect life in eternal communion with God. Paul announces the resurrection of Jesus in the conviction that "the one who raised the Lord Jesus will raise us also with Jesus, and will bring us with you into his presence" (2 Cor 4:14).

2.6 The Easter Accounts

119. One specific difficulty regarding the historical truth of the Easter accounts derives from the fact that in them we find many differences that are not easily harmonized from the purely factual point of view. The event itself of Jesus' resurrection is not described in any New Testament text; it is hidden, in fact, from human eyes

and belongs exclusively to the mystery of God. We have instead two types of Easter accounts which narrate what happened after the resurrection: the visit of some women to the tomb of Jesus and the various appearances of the risen Lord (cf. also 1 Cor 15:3-8) who showed himself alive to witnesses chosen by him. The visit to the tomb is the only paschal event for which we have a similar account in all four gospels, although with numerous variations in detail.

We wish to consider in particular three differences which, among others, may be seen in the four accounts: (a) only Matthew 28:2 mentions an earthquake before speaking of the arrival of the women at Jesus' tomb; (b) only Mark 16:8 speaks of the women fleeing, afraid and silent after the encounter with the heavenly messenger; and (c) according to the Synoptics (Matt 28:5-7; Mark 16:6-7; Luke 24:5-7), the message of Jesus' resurrection was delivered to the women by one or more messengers of God; according to John 20:14-17, on the other hand, Mary Magdalene, although seeing two angels in the tomb (John 20:12-13), receives directly from Jesus the proclamation of his resurrection.

2.6.1 The Earthquake

120. The fact that only Matthew 28:2 speaks of an earthquake does not mean that the other gospels deny it by failing to mention it. Such a deduction would not be reliable, since it is based exclusively on an argument *e silentio*. On the other hand, the "earthquake" seems to be part of theological style of Matthew. Only this Evangelist, in fact, mentions an earthquake—together with other extraordinary phenomena—after the death of Jesus (27:51-53), and he presents it as the reason why the centurion and his soldiers are filled with fear and confess the divine sonship of Jesus crucified (27:54). In relation to this, one must bear in mind that an earthquake is one of the phenomena in which the presence and activity of God manifest themselves in many Old Testament descriptions of theophanies (cf. Exod 19:18; Judg 5:4-5; 1 Kgs 19:11; Pss 18:8; 68:8-9; 97:4; Isa 63:19). In the book of Revelation, the earthquake symbolically indicates an upheaval which leads to the fall of the "earthly structure," constituted by a world which, built outside of

God and in opposition to God, at a certain point collapses (cf. Rev 6:12; 11:13; 16:18).

It is likely, therefore, that Matthew uses this "literary motif." By mentioning the earthquake, he wishes to underline that the death and resurrection of Jesus are not ordinary events but "traumatic" events in which God acts and achieves the salvation of the human race. The specific meaning of the divine action must be inferred from the context of the gospel: the death of Jesus accomplishes the forgiveness of sins and reconciliation with God (cf. Matt 20:28; 26:28), and in his resurrection, Jesus overcomes death, enters into the life of God the Father, and obtains power over all (cf. 28:18-20). The Evangelist does not speak, then, of an earthquake whose force could be measured according to the grades of a specific scale but seeks to awaken and direct the attention of his readers toward God, highlighting the most important fact about the death and resurrection of Jesus: their relationship with the saving power of God.

2.6.2 The Behavior of the Women

121. A similar situation is to be found in Mark 16:8, which recounts the reaction of the women to the paschal message, a reaction of fear and bewilderment: "So they went out and fled from the tomb, for terror and amazement had seized them; and they said nothing to anyone, for they were afraid." The other evangelists do not speak of such behavior. Just as the earthquake is one of the phenomena which accompany the manifestation of God's power, so too fear represents the usual human reaction to such a manifestation. It is characteristic of the Gospel of Mark to express through the reaction of those present the nature and character of events at which they have assisted (cf. 1:22, 27; 4:41; 5:42; etc.). The strongest and most marked reaction recounted in his gospel is that of the women after hearing the paschal message from the messenger of God. Through their reaction, the Evangelist underlines that the resurrection of the crucified Jesus is the greatest manifestation of the saving power of God. The Evangelist not only communicates the event as such but also points to its specific relevance for human beings and the effect produced upon them.

2.6.3 The Source of the Easter Message

122. The source of the Easter message is presented in different ways by the gospels. According to the Synoptics (Matt 28:5-7; Mark 16:6-7; Luke 24:5-7), the women who go to Jesus' tomb and find it empty receive from one or two heavenly envoys the message about Jesus' resurrection. According to John 20:1-2, however, Mary Magdalene, after finding the tomb empty, runs to the disciples and says to them: "They have taken the Lord out of the tomb, and we do not know where they have laid him." She repeats her explanation of the empty tomb two more times (20:13, 15), and only after the appearance of the risen Lord himself (20:14-17) does she bring the message of the resurrection to the disciples (20:18). One may ask if Matthew, Mark, and Luke, in mentioning the discovery of the empty tomb, anticipate the true interpretation of this event, in contrast to that mentioned above given by Mary Magdalene in John 20:2, 13, 15 (cf. also Matt 28:13). By placing this explanation in the mouth of a heavenly messenger, the three evangelists characterize it as superhuman knowledge which can only come from God. But the effective source of such an interpretation is the risen Lord himself, who appears to chosen witnesses. There is no doubt that his appearances provide the firmest foundation of faith in the resurrection of Jesus (cf. also 1 Cor 15:3-8).

The four accounts of the visit to the tomb, with their differences, make a historical harmonization rather difficult, but these very divergences constitute for us a true stimulus to understand them more properly. The study of their three principal differences—the earthquake, the women's flight, the heavenly message—brings out their common significance; they testify to God and to the decisive intervention of his saving power in the resurrection of Jesus. This result, if, on the one hand, free from the constraint of having to see in every detail of the narrative—not only of the Easter accounts, but of the whole gospels—a precise record, on the other hand, it compels us to remain open and attentive to the theological meaning of both the differences and the details of the account.

2.6.4 The "Theological Value of the Gospels"

123. The opinion that the gospels are essentially a chronicle of facts, of which the witnesses furnish an exact account, is still a widespread opinion. This idea is based on the just conviction that the Christian faith is not ahistorical speculation but is founded on events that really happened. God acts in history and shows his presence in an eminent way in that of his incarnate Son. But a view which sees the gospels solely as a type of chronicle can lose sight of their theological significance and thereby overlook all their richness precisely as a word which speaks of God. Already in its 1964 Instruction *Sancta Mater Ecclesia* regarding the historical truth of the gospels the Pontifical Biblical Commission declared: "Based on new studies, it follows that the life and teaching of Jesus were not simply presented with the sole end of preserving a record, but were rather 'preached' so as to offer the basis for the faith and traditions of the Church. For this reason, the exegete, diligently scrutinizing the witnesses of the evangelists, will be able to illustrate the perennial value of the Gospel with greater insight, and to cast in full light what is the necessity and importance of the Church's interpretation" (*EB* 652).

We must, therefore, bear in mind the fact that the gospels are not merely chronicles of the events in the life of Jesus, since the evangelists also intend to express in narrative form the theological significance of these events. This signifies that they, in all their narrations, do not mean to recount only events; they also intend to make a "theological comment" on the facts which they are recounting to bring out their theological significance, especially their relationship with God.

In other words, the intention of announcing Jesus, the Son of God and Savior of all—an intention which can be called "theological"—is widespread and fundamental in the gospels. The reference to concrete facts which we encounter in the gospels falls within the framework of this theological announcement. This means that while the theological affirmations about Jesus have a direct and normative import, the purely historical elements have a subordinate function.

III. Second Challenge: Ethical and Social Problems

124. Other biblical texts, of a different kind, present a challenge for their interpretation. These recount positively immoral forms of behavior which express sentiments of hatred and violence or seem to promote social conditions considered unjust today. These texts can scandalize and disorient Christians, who at times feel themselves accused by non-Christians of having in their sacred book the features of a religion which teaches immorality and violence. For this difficult discussion, we have chosen, in the case of the Old Testament, to face the question of violence, expressed particularly in the law of extermination (the ban) and in the Psalms which demand vengeance; for the New Testament, we will look at the social status of women in the letters of Paul.

3.1 Violence in the Bible

125. One of the major obstacles to the reception of the Bible as inspired Word is the presence, especially in the Old Testament, of repeated cases of violence and cruelty, in many cases, commanded by God; in many others, the object of prayers addressed to the Lord; in others still, directly attributed to him by the sacred author.

The discomfort of the contemporary reader should not be minimized. It has, in fact, led some to assume a disapproving attitude toward some Old Testament texts, considered outdated and inadequate to nurture faith. The Catholic hierarchy was aware of the pastoral implications of the problem, deciding that entire biblical passages are not read in the public liturgy while systematically omitting those verses which would be offensive to Christian sensibilities. One could improperly deduce from this that a part of Sacred Scripture does not enjoy the charism of inspiration, since it would not be "useful for teaching, for reproof, correction, and for training in righteousness" (2 Tim 3:16).

It is essential, therefore, to indicate a few rules of interpretation that would render a more acceptable approach to the biblical tradition possible, in the case of its problematic texts; these, in any case, will have to be interpreted in the overall context of Scripture, that is, in the light of the Gospel message of love even for one's enemies (Matt 5:38-48).

3.1.1 Violence and Its Legal Remedies

126. From its opening pages, the Bible presents the occurrence of violence in human society (Gen 4:8, 23-24; 6:11, 13), the origin of which lies in the rejection of God which takes the form of idolatry (Rom 1:18-32). Sacred Scripture denounces and condemns every form of oppression, from slavery to fratricidal wars, from personal assaults to oppressive systems, whether between nations or within Israel (Amos 1:3–2:16). Placing the fearful consequences of a perverted heart before the eyes of all (Gen 6:5; Jer 17:1), the Word of God has a prophetic function: in this way it invites us to recognize evil in order to avoid and resist it.

To promote knowledge of the good to be accomplished (Rom 3:20) and to facilitate the process of conversion, Scripture proclaims the law of God, which acts as a brake on the spread of injustice. The Torah of the Lord, however, does not indicate solely the way of righteousness which everyone is duty-bound to follow, but it also prescribes which actions are to be employed against wrongdoers, so that evil may be purged (Deut 17:12; 22:21, 22, 24; etc.), victims may be recompensed, and peace may be promoted. Such a disposition cannot be criticized as violent. The punitive sanction is in fact necessary, because not only does it highlight the iniquity and danger of the crime but, in addition to establishing a just retribution, it targets the correction of the guilty person and, by instilling the fear of punishment, helps society and the individual to abstain from wrongdoing. To abolish punishment entirely would be the equivalent of tolerating the misdeed, becoming complicit in it. The penal system, regulated by the so-called law of retaliation ("eye for eye, tooth for tooth": Exod 21:24; Lev 24:20; Deut 19:21), thus constitutes a reasonable means of furthering the common good. Although imperfect because of its coercive aspects and some of its ways of punishment, this system is actually taken over, with appropriate adjustments, by legal systems of every era and country, because it is ideally based on the equal proportion between crime and punishment, between damage inflicted and damage suffered. Instead of an arbitrary vendetta, the limits of a just response to an evil act are set.

One could object that some punitive measures envisaged in the Old Testament law codes appear unbearably cruel (such as flogging: Deut 25:1-3; or mutilation: Deut 25:11-12), and even the death penalty, stipulated for the most serious crimes, is widely opposed today. In cases such as these, the reader of the Bible must, on the one hand, recognize the historical character of the biblical legislation, outdated by a better understanding of the procedures of justice more respectful of the inalienable rights of the person; on the other hand, the ancient prescriptions can in any event serve to point out the gravity of certain crimes which require appropriate measures to avoid the spread of evil.

When in Sacred Scripture the author attributes to God and the human judge the display of indignation while administering punitive justice, improper behavior is not envisaged here; it is imperative, in fact, that evil not remain unpunished, and it is appropriate that the victims be aided and compensated. On the other hand, Scripture, even in the Old Testament, completes the idea of God as guarantor of justice with the repeated recollection of his great patience (Exod 34:6; Num 14:18; Ps 103:8; etc.) and, above all, with the continual openness to forgiveness for the sinner (Isa 1:18; Gen 4:11), forgiveness granted when feelings and actions of true repentance appear (Gen 3:10; Ezek 18:23). The divine model, which mitigates the necessary rigor of discipline through meekness and the hope of forgiveness, is proposed for imitation in the Bible to persons responsible for justice and social harmony.

3.1.2 The Law of Extermination

127. In the book of Deuteronomy, in particular, we read that God commands Israel to overthrow the Canaanite nations and put them under the curse of destruction (Deut 7:1-2; 20:16-18); the order is faithfully executed by Joshua (Josh 6–12) and brought to completion in the first monarchical period (cf. 1 Sam 15). This whole literary presentation is especially problematic, even more than all the wars and massacres narrated in the Old Testament; to offer it as a program

of nationalistic political conduct, justifying violence against other nations, is in any case decidedly blameworthy, because it distorts the meaning of the biblical message.

From the outset, it is necessary to note that these narratives do not have the characteristics of a historical account: in a real war, in fact, the walls of a city do not come crashing down at the sound of trumpets (Josh 6:20), nor is it evident how a peaceful distribution of lands by lottery could really take place (Josh 14:2). On the other hand, the norm in Deuteronomy which prescribes the extermination of the Canaanites takes written form at a moment in history when these populations were no longer identifiable in the land of Israel. One must, therefore, reconsider carefully the literary genre of these narrative traditions. As the best interpreters of the patristic tradition had already suggested, the narration of the conquest epic should be seen as a sort of parable presenting characters of symbolic value; the law of extermination, for its part, requires a nonliteral interpretation, as in the case of the command of the Lord to cut off one's hand or pluck out one's eye, if they are a cause of scandal (Matt 5:29; 18:9).

We must still indicate, however, how one could orient the reading of these difficult passages. The first controversial aspect of the literary tradition just mentioned is the *conquest*, understood as the ousting of the inhabitants of a place and their replacement by the conquerors. The appeal to God's right to distribute the land, thus privileging his own elect (Deut 7:6-11; 32:8-9), is certainly not convincing, because it disavows the legitimate claims of the native populations. Other, more convincing approaches are in fact furnished by the biblical text itself. In the first place, the account presents the conflict between two groups of different economic and military strength: that of the Canaanites, very powerful (Deut 7:1; see also Num 13:33; Deut 1:28; Amos 2:9; etc.), and that of the Israelites, weak and defenseless; what is not presented here, therefore, as the ideal model, is the triumph of the powerful, but, on the contrary, the triumph of the little one, corresponding to a "type" well-attested throughout the Bible down to the New Testament (Luke 1:52; 1 Cor 1:27). This represents a prophetic reading of history, which sees in the victory of the "meek" in a "holy" war the fulfillment of the Kingdom of God on earth. Moreover, according to what is attested in the Bible, the Canaanites are seen by God as guilty of very serious crimes (Gen 15:16; Lev 18:3, 24-30; 20:23; Deut 9:4-5; etc.), among which is the killing of their own children in perverted rituals (Deut 12:31; 18:10-12). The narrative, then, holds out the prospect of the execution of divine justice in history. And Joshua shows himself to be "the servant of the Lord" (Josh 24:29; Jdg 2:8) in taking on the task of carrying out justice: his victories are consistently attributed to the Lord and to his superhuman power. So the literary motif of judgment upon the nations begins in the accounts of origin, but, as is documented by the prophets and the apocalyptic writings, it will be extended to various peoples whenever a nation—and thus also Israel—is adjudged by God worthy of punishment.

It is, therefore, along these lines that the *law of extermination* and its precise application on the part of the faithful of the Lord must be understood. Such legislation is prompted by the view of the sacredness of the people of the Covenant (Deut 7:6), which must signify, with a behavior that may be extreme, that they are radically different from other nations. God certainly does not command them to commit an outrage which would be justified on religious grounds; he calls on them to obey a duty of justice similar to the prosecution, condemnation, and execution of a criminal guilty of a capital crime, be it an individual or a community. Showing mercy, sparing the criminal, is considered an act of disobedience and an injustice (Deut 13:9-10; 19:13, 21; 25:12; 1 Sam 15:18-19; 1 Kgs 20:42). In this case also, therefore, the apparently violent action is to be interpreted as concern to remove evil and thus to safeguard the common good. This literary trend is corrected by others—among which is the so-called priestly tendency—which, regarding the same facts, advocates an approach of extreme pacifism. For this reason, we must understand the entire event of the conquest as a sort of symbol, analogous to what we read in certain gospel parables of judgment (Matt 13:30, 41-43, 50; 25:30, 41; etc.). This story, we repeat, must, in any event, be integrated with other biblical passages which announce the compassion and forgiveness of God as the scope and goal of every historical action of the Lord of all the earth, as well as the model for just actions on the part of human beings.

3.1.3 The Prayer Calling for Vengeance

128. The manifestation of violence is particularly inconvenient when it occurs in prayer, yet in the Psalter itself we find expressions of hatred and desire for vengeance which contrast radically with the sentiments of love for one's enemies taught by the Lord Jesus to his disciples (Matt 5:44; Luke 6:27, 35). While respecting the prudent decision to omit from the liturgy those passages which could give rise to scandal, it is appropriate to give some indications which will allow believers even today, as happened in the past, to make the entire patrimony of Israel's prayer their own.

The primary way to explain and accept the difficult expressions in the Psalms is that of understanding their *literary genre*; this means that the turns of phrase we meet there are not to be taken literally. In the prayers of supplication and lament made by a person who is persecuted, the "imprecatory" motif appears frequently; it presents itself as a passionate supplication to God for salvation through the elimination of the enemy. In certain psalms, this vindictive dimension becomes insistent or even dominant (as in Ps 109). If the formulations used by the Psalmist are linguistically moderate (for example, "Let them be turned back and confounded who devise evil against me": Ps 35:4), they may be more easily integrated into prayer; brutal images, on the other hand, become problematic or unacceptable, images such as "In your steadfast love cut off my enemies, and destroy all my adversaries" (Ps 143:12) or "O Daughter Babylon, . . . happy shall they be who take your little ones and dash them against the rock!" (Ps 137:8-9). In this regard three aspects are to be considered.

a) The One Who Prays: The Suffering Person

129. The literary genre of the lament makes use of exaggerated and exasperated expressions, both in its description of suffering, which is always extreme ("They have pierced my hands and feet; I can count all my bones" [Ps 22:17-18; RSV]; "More in number than the hairs of my head are those who hate me without cause" [Ps 69:4]), and in the request for remedies, which should be swift

and definitive. This is motivated by the fact that such a prayer expresses the emotional state of mind of those who find themselves in a dramatic situation; their feelings, therefore, cannot be composed, and their words resemble a roar (Ps 22:2). In any case, the images employed should be regarded as metaphors: "break the teeth of the wicked" (Ps 3:7; 58:7) means to put an end to the lies and greed of the overbearing; "smash their children against the rock" means to annihilate, without the possibility of their reproducing in the future, the malignant forces which destroy life; and so on. Moreover, the one who prays the Psalter uses words written by another person in different circumstances; one must, for this reason, make a transposition in order to apply those words to one's own personal experience. A similar actualization will be more successful, if one uses the prayer of lament not as expressive (only) of one's own personal situation but as the pained voice of the victims of the whole of history, like the cry of the martyrs (Rev 6:10) who plead with God that the violent "beast" be removed forever from the earth.

b) What Does the One Praying Request? "Deliver Us from Evil"

130. In the imprecatory prayer, no magical action is performed which would have a direct effect on one's enemies; instead the person praying entrusts to God the task of administering that justice which no one on earth can. There is in this the renunciation of personal vengeance (Rom 12:19; Heb 10:30), and, moreover, in this way, one expresses confidence in a response of the Lord that is proportionate to the gravity of the situation, in full conformity with the very nature of God. The expressions used by the person who prays seem to dictate to God the way to act; but understood correctly, they speak only of the desire that evil may be destroyed, so that the humble may have life. And it is requested that this should happen in history, as a manifestation of the Lord (Pss 35:27; 59:14; 109:27) and, as a consequence, a mediation that leads to conversion of the violent themselves (Pss 9:21; 83:18-19). In fact, the persecution against the one who prays is seen in certain cases as an aggression against God (Pss 2:2; 83:3, 13), often accompanied by contempt for the Lord (Pss 10:4, 13; 42:4; 73:11).

c) Who Are the Enemies of the One Praying?

131. Identifying the enemies of the one praying is not merely an exegetical matter that would reveal the figures and the historical occasions to which the sacred author may have alluded. In reality, the situation described in the Psalms (of lament) is for the most part stereotypical: the language is conventional and often deliberately metaphorical, so that it can be applied to various circumstances and to different types of subject. A "prophetic" act of interpretation in the Spirit is necessary, therefore, to be able to see how the Psalmist's words apply in the concrete life of the person reciting a psalm of lament and in this very circumstance to recognize who the threatening enemy may be (as in Acts 4:23-30).

Progress is made in identifying the enemy when it is discovered that the enemy is not merely the one who threatens the physical life or dignity of the person praying but rather the one who threatens that person's spiritual life (Matt 10:28). What are the hostile forces which the believer must confront? Who, or what, is the "roaring lion" (Ps 22:13; 1 Pet 5:8) or the "poisonous tongue of the serpent" (Ps 140:3), for which one should have an implacable hatred (Pss 26:5; 139:21-22) and whose annihilation is sought from God (Ps 31:18)? "Our struggle is not against enemies of blood and flesh," Saint Paul writes (Eph 6:12); it is from the evil one, who is "Legion" (Mark 5:9), that the person praying begs to be delivered, as by an exorcism, through the powerful mercy of God. And, as in every exorcism, the words are harsh, because they express the absolute hostility between God and evil, between the sons of God and the world of sin (Jas 4:4).

3.2 The Social Status of Women

132. A number of biblical passages, especially Pauline, invite us to reflect on what, in the canon of the Old Testament as also in that of the New, should be considered perennially valid and what should be considered relative, linked to a culture, a civilization, or even the mentality of a specific period of time. The status of women in the Pauline epistles raises this type of question.

3.2.1 The Submission of Wives to Their Husbands

In the letters to the Colossians (3:18), Ephesians (5:22-33), and Titus (2:5), Paul asks wives to submit themselves to their husbands; in doing so, he is following Greek and Jewish customs of his time, according to which women had an inferior social status to that of men. The exhortation appears not to follow Galatians 3:28, where he declares that there must not be discrimination in the Church, neither between Jews and Greeks, nor between slaves and free, nor between men and women.

In the passages of Ephesians and Colossians, the submission of the wife is based not on social norms in place at that time but rather on the conduct of the husband, a conduct that has its origin in *agape*, whose model is the love of Christ himself for his Body, the Church. Nevertheless, Paul has been accused of invoking this supreme example the more easily to keep the wife in subjection and, in doing so, to subject Christians to worldly values—in other words, a detachment from the Gospel!

To these objections, we respond by saying that Paul insists not on the submission of wives (the reasons for this are very brief) but rather on the love which the husband should show toward his wife, a love which for Paul is the condition not only of the union and unity of the couple but also of the submission and homage of the wife to her husband. The superiority of the husband's social status, which constitutes the first motive (Eph 5:23), disappears completely from the scene at the end of the argument. What must be retained, therefore, is the manner in which Paul, independently of a fixed role for each of the spouses in the society of the time, seeks to promote the renewal of the behavior of the husband, whose status was socially superior. Moreover, the submission of the wife to her husband must never be separated from Ephesians 5:21, where Paul says that all believers must "be subject to one another."

Nevertheless, one difficulty remains. What use does a Christological and ecclesial model serve if it does not point to the fact that the inferior rank of the wife is not appropriate within the Church, since all believers have the same dignity and the same Lord, Christ? That Paul could have compromised himself with worldly values must be excluded. To tell the truth, he does not propose new social models, but without materially modifying those of his time, he invites the interiorization of relationships or social rules considered stable and enduring at a certain period—that of the first century—so that they can be lived in conformity with the Gospel.

Many centuries later, we can still regret that Paul in these letters did not clearly assert equality of social status for believing spouses, but his way of proceeding was perhaps the only one possible at that time; otherwise, Christianity could have been accused of undermining the social order. On the other hand, though, the exhortation to husbands has not lost any of its actuality and its truth.

3.2.2 The Silence of Women in Ecclesial Gatherings

133. The passage in 1 Corinthians 14:33-35 also raises difficulties, because Paul calls on women to remain silent during the assemblies: "As in all the churches of the saints, women should be silent in the churches. For they are not permitted to speak, but should be subordinate, as the law also says. If there is anything they desire to know, let them ask their husbands at home. For it is shameful for a woman to speak in church." These verses seem to contradict 1 Corinthians 14:31 ("You can all prophesy") and 1 Corinthians 11:5, which speak of women prophesying during the assemblies. But the pronouncements of 1 Corinthians 14:33-35 must be contextualized, that is, interpreted in relation to the preceding verses on prophecy. Paul certainly does not intend to say that women are not authorized to prophesy (cf. 11:5) but that they must not evaluate and judge the prophecies of their husbands in the assembly (14:29). The principles underlying such a prohibition are those of respect, harmony between spouses, and good order in the assemblies. If these principles still apply today, their application evidently depends on the *status* granted to women in particular societies and cultures. Paul does not turn the silence of women into an absolute but only a means corresponding to the situation of the assemblies of that time. And today, we must not confuse the principles and their application, which is always determined by the social and cultural context.

3.2.3 The Role of Women in the Assembly

134. More difficult and less defensible, if understood as an absolute principle, is the way in which 1 Timothy 2:11-15 justifies the inferior status of women in social and ecclesial contexts: "Let a woman learn in silence with full submission. I permit no woman to teach or to have authority over a man; she is to keep silent. For Adam was formed first, then Eve; and Adam was not deceived, but the woman was deceived and became a transgressor. Yet she will be saved through childbearing, provided they continue in faith and love and holiness, with modesty." The context is that of the ecclesial assemblies, composed of men and women. Paul does not call on women to be silent, nor does he prevent them from prophesying; the prohibition refers only to teaching and the charisms of governance. The idea is more or less the same as in the preceding cases: teaching and governance were at that time reserved for men, and Paul wishes that this social order, considered natural in that time period, be respected (cf. 1 Cor 11:3: "the husband is the head of his wife").

It is not so much this idea that raises difficulty, for, as was said above, it could be adapted to the culture and society in which one lives, but rather the way in which it is justified, that is, by means of a problematic interpretation of the accounts of Genesis 2–3: the order of creation (the man has a superior status, since he was created before the woman; cf. Gen 2:18-24) and the fall of the woman in Paradise. Now, the interpretation of Genesis 3 found in 1 Timothy is already present in Sirach 25:24 and in other writings, as, for example, in the Jewish apocryphal work *The Life of Adam and Eve* or *The Apocalypse of Moses* in its Greek translation. The woman allowed herself to be deceived by the serpent, sinned, and was responsible for the death of all the human species; she must, therefore, behave with modesty and not seek to dominate the man. This reading is clearly influenced by the way in which one conceived and justified at the time the respective social status of men and women; moreover, it is not compatible with 1 Corinthians 15:21-22 and Romans 5:12-21; it also reflects an ecclesial situation in which one needed to find authoritative arguments to respond to women who lamented that they could not take on the above mentioned roles in the ecclesial assemblies. It is evident that this reading of Genesis 2–3 is conditioned by the circumstances of the first century. A correct interpretation of a biblical passage—here Genesis 2–3—must nevertheless understand and respect the *intentio textus*.

IV. Conclusion

135. The assertion that the Bible communicates the Word of God seems to be disproved by more than a few biblical passages. We have examined two types of texts: narratives which appear to be improbable and incapable of standing up to a serious historical-scientific investigation and passages which not only propose but impose behavior that is immoral, or that contradicts social justice. We will now present a brief synthesis of the results of our investigation and seek to formulate a few consequences for a more appropriate reading and a more correct understanding of the biblical texts.

4.1 Brief Synthesis

The study of four Old Testament accounts have shown that a reading which is solely interested in facts that actually happened is unable to grasp the intention and content of these texts. In the case of Genesis 15 and Exodus 14, the events recounted cannot be verified with precision by historical science. For the narrators of these texts, the survival of their people over the centuries is a historical fact, and their faith in God is decisive in their situation and experience (the time of exile). Their accounts attest that the fundamental attitude is unconditional faith in God and in his unlimited saving power. In the case of Tobit and Jonah, we noted that texts which do not recount what really happened are nevertheless accounts full of edifying, didactic, and theological significance.

With regard to the narrative texts of the New Testament, it was shown that interest in historical facts does not suffice; one must pay close attention to the meaning of what is recounted. In the infancy narratives, not all details of the accounts can be verified historically, while the virginal conception of Jesus is clearly affirmed. These accounts introduce us to the rest of the written work, presenting the principal characteristics of the person and work of Jesus. The miracles (works of power, signs), for their part, are present in all the traditions relating to the activity of Jesus. Their significance does not consist solely in the fact that they are extraordinary deeds. In the Synoptic Gospels, they indicate the salvific presence of the Kingdom of God in the person and work of Jesus; in John they reveal the relationship between Jesus and God and lead to faith in Jesus (cf. also Matt 8:27; 14:33). The Easter accounts, precisely because of their divergences, show that they are not simple chronicles; they attract attention because of the theologically important details of the accounts.

The explanation of the law of extermination and of the prayer which calls for vengeance situated these texts in their historical and literal context, allowing their significance and usefulness to be better understood. The particulars on the status of women in the Pauline epistles highlight the need to distinguish between the principles of true Christian behavior and their application in the cultural and social context of the time.

4.2 Some Consequences for the Reading of the Bible

136. At first glance, many narrative texts of the Bible appear to have the character of a precise record of what actually happened. Corresponding to this impression is a way of reading the Bible which sees in all the events recounted things that really occurred. This manner of reading seems to allow an approach to the content of the Bible that is simple, immediate, possible for all, with clear and sure results.

On the contrary, the reading of Scripture which takes account of the modern sciences (historiography, philology, archeology, cultural anthropology, etc.) complicates the understanding of the biblical texts and appears to propose less certain results. We cannot, however, ignore demands of our time and interpret the texts of the Bible outside their historical context; we must read them in our time, with and for our contemporaries. The course followed in this document shows how a search for the meaning of the texts that goes beyond the preoccupation of determining merely the facts that actually happened leads to a more profound and precise understanding of their sense.

When one does not find in the biblical accounts the chronicle-type report of narrated facts, there is the danger, to be carefully avoided, that one concludes from this that everything in the Bible is invented, produced by human ideas and beliefs. God reveals himself in history, his "plan of revelation is realized by deeds and words having an inner unity" (*DV*, n. 2). It is the task of the Bible to transmit these deeds and words. It is the task of a serious and appropriate reading of the Bible to be attentive to these deeds and words.

The presence of the law of extermination and of similar texts brings to light another important element for reading the Bible. This recounts the history of God's revelation and, at the same time, the history of revealed moral behavior. As the revelation of God, so also the revelation of just human conduct reaches its fullness in Jesus. Just as we cannot find in every single biblical passage the full revelation of God, so too, we cannot find the perfect revelation of morality. Single passages of Scripture, therefore, must not be isolated or absolutized but must be understood and evaluated in their relationship with the fullness of revelation in the person and work of Jesus and in the framework of a canonical reading of Sacred Scripture. A profound understanding of these texts in themselves is very helpful; in this way the history of revelation itself is manifested.

Finally, it is fundamental that the orientation of the reader of Sacred Scripture is that of seeking what it says about God and the salvation of human beings. In doing so, even if one does not always reach an adequate understanding of the text being read, one will nevertheless make continuing progress in the knowledge of the truth of the Bible, in the spiritual wisdom that is the way toward full communion with God.

General Conclusion

137. With a solemn and normative pronouncement at the Council of Trent (*EB*, 58–60), the Catholic Church accepted the canon of sacred books, thus defining the fundamental parameters of its belief. The Church set forth which texts are to be regarded as written "under the inspiration of the Holy Spirit" (*DV*, n. 11) and therefore indispensable for the formation and edification of the believer and the entire Christian community (cf. 2 Tim 3:15-16). If, on the one hand, one is fully aware that these writings were composed by human authors who left on them the stamp of their own particular literary genius, on the other hand, one equally recognizes in them a unique divine quality variously attested by the sacred texts and variously explained by theologians over the course of history.

138. The task of the Biblical Commission, charged with expressing itself on this matter, is not to formulate a doctrine of inspiration in competition with what is usually presented in manuals of systematic theology. The Commission, by means of this document, aims to show how Sacred Scripture itself points to the divine provenance of its assertions, thus becoming the messenger of God's truth. We place ourselves, therefore, in a context of faith: we welcome, in fact, what the Church passes down to us as the Word of God, and from this Word we draw elements of understanding that favor a more mature reception of this divine inheritance.

139. The Sacred Scriptures form a unified whole, because all the books, "with all their parts," possess the character of an inspired text, since they have God himself "as their author" (*DV*, n. 11). Nevertheless, although acknowledging that every word of the sacred text can

be considered the Word of God, consistent with all the others, yet the Church has always recognized an aspect of multiplicity, which can seem to be in contrast with its unique divine origin. The distinction between Old and New Testaments is the clearest manifestation of important differences within the Bible itself. In the ancient Christian basilicas, two lecterns were placed for the reading of the sacred texts to signify the distinction and the complementarity of the two Testaments, both necessary to attest the unique event of the definitive revelation consisting in the mystery of Christ the Lord. In this contribution of ours, too, we have respected the nature proper to each of the constitutive parts of Sacred Scripture, showing that their diversity not only does not gainsay but rather enriches the true testimony of the one Word of God.

Within the two main parts of the Bible, the variety of literary genres, theological categories, and anthropological and sociological approaches is also particularly evident. God has spoken, in fact, "in many and various ways" (Heb 1:1), not only in ancient times, but also after the coming of the Son who fully revealed the Father (cf. John 1:18). It seemed our duty, then, in this document to illustrate with appropriate surveys such a rich diversity of assertions, all imbued with the same conviction that they are expressing the divine truth.

I. The Divine Provenance of the Biblical Writings

140. The believing community lives by a tradition: in fact, it feels itself constituted by listening to the Word of God, committed to writing in some books, handed on as normative, insofar as they bear within themselves the stamp of their authority.

This was guaranteed above all by the authority of the writers who, according to an ancient and venerable tradition, were recognized as sent by God and endowed with the charism of inspiration. Thus, through many centuries up to modern times, the literary paternity of the Pentateuch, attributed as a whole to Moses, was not questioned; nor that of various prophetic and wisdom books, which, when they lacked a specific title, were assigned to well-known authors (such as David, Solomon, Jeremiah, etc.).

This traditional form of reception was followed also for the New Testament writings, which were all seen as coming from the inner circle of the apostles. Today, thanks to the converging results of researchers using literary and historical methodologies, we cannot maintain the same perspective as the ancients; the science of exegesis has actually demonstrated with convincing arguments that the various biblical writings are not the exclusive product of the author indicated in the work's title or recognized as such by the tradition. The literary history of the Bible postulates, rather, a plurality of interventions and, therefore, a collaboration of different authors, for the most part anonymous, throughout a rather long and trying period of redaction. This obligatory employment of an interpretive model in relation to the origin of the sacred writings is not diametrically opposed to the traditional concept, sometimes hastily censured as hermeneutical naivety. The Church, in fact, in its patient and painstaking work of discernment carried on for several centuries, has always understood that it could receive as inspired those writings which were consistent with the deposit of faith firmly and faithfully preserved by the believing community, guaranteed by those whom God had selected as shepherds and guides for the faithful. The Spirit at work in the Church, with its characteristic power of discernment, permitted what was an authentic divine communication to be distinguished from false or insufficiently established forms. In certain cases, then, a text which bore the name of an inspired individual was rejected, while a writing was received with veneration which, though not guaranteed by the signature of a recognized author, nevertheless bore the unmistakable imprint of one. With an extraordinary awareness of the truth of revelation, the Church defines herself in the obedient recognition of the Word of God by which she lives.

1.1 In Consonance with the Word

141. The Church bases its entire discernment on the living experience of the Lord Jesus, received in the word of the witnesses who knew him and recognized in him the accomplishment of divine revelation. Beginning from what the apostles and evangelists proclaimed,

the canon of sacred books was gradually established, and the Church saw in their various attestations the character of authentic truth, since it was in harmony with the testimony on the Son of God. It was not because a particular writing presented itself claiming to be the Word of God that it was entitled to be read in the liturgical assemblies as a basis of faith, but rather because, in its message, it was consistent with the Word and constituted an appropriate explanation of that Word. It is this *consistency*, in the very variety of expression and in the plurality of theologies, that is illustrated in the pages of this document through the exploration of the diverse self-testimonies furnished by the books of Sacred Scripture.

Such an accord is not limited to a generic convergence of some fundamental doctrines. If it were, this would diminish the respect for the diversity of perspectives, for the irreducible complementarity of every contribution, and for the literary history of these books born from the assimilation and innovative restating of ancient materials. The sacred writer, in fact, according to the very attestation of Jesus, draws out from his treasure the new along with the old (cf. Matt 13:52). This signifies that the writings recognized by Church as inspired not only claim their provenance from God in a more or less explicit way but attest, at the same time, the authenticity of the writings which preceded them. The prophets validate the law, and the wisdom writings recognize the divine origin of the law and the prophets; in an analogous way, the testimony of Jesus consecrates the entire written tradition of the Hebrew people, and the writings of the New Testament confirm each other, absorbing all the traditions of the ancient Scriptures in a radical and consonant way.

II. The Plurality of the Modes of Attestation

142. This is one of the principal results obtained by the analysis of different books of the Old and New Testaments conducted in the present document. Alongside this aspect of significant convergence there emerged clearly the *plurality* of religious experiences and of formulations which they transmitted. It is not possible to take up again here, in a detailed and exhaustive manner, the ways in which the various biblical authors point to the divine provenance of their

words; suffice it to point to some models which, with different emphases, are to be found in various books of Sacred Scripture.

The most important manner of self-witness is that expressed in the accounts of the prophetic call and in the various formulae which are found throughout the pages of the prophets. Here the reality of inspiration is formally expressed as the intimate awareness of some men who declare that they are able to understand the words of God and have received the mandate to transmit them faithfully. This model, because of its suggestive force, was borrowed by other sacred authors of the legislative (Moses), wisdom (Solomon), and apocalyptic (Daniel) traditions, thus creating a kind of general uniformity, almost like a seal of guarantee to confirm for the readers the nature of the writing as deriving from a single divine source.

143. In an equally diffuse way, the Bible presents the active participation of collaborators of the inspired author, endowed with literary competence and positive reliability; these not only assisted the principal authors but also gathered together new material, adapted previous material to the new demands of the addressees, and carried out, generation after generation, an impressive redactional work of decisive importance for the quality of the biblical text. The prophetic charism was certainly active in these anonymous redactors, who indirectly attest their awareness of transmitting the words of the Lord in the very act of handing over the writings marked with their specific contribution.

Biblical scholars have reasonably conjectured the existence of currents, schools, and religious groups capable of guarding, in a viable way, literary traditions considered sacred and which later flowed into the channel of Sacred Scripture, so that—although pointing out the usefulness of determining a history of the composition of biblical texts—one cannot and must not attribute either a different value or a different authority to that which was "original" compared to that which has a secondary origin.

In many cases, in fact, we do not have the *ipsissima verba* of the prophet (inspired by God), unless in the words of his disciples. This is typically the case in the gospels, whose inspiration is not in question; in this genre of writing the author (that is, the Evangelist) presents himself as a faithful witness of the Master and, in certain cases, as a disciple of his first disciples (not being mentioned in the list of apostles).

From these indications the necessity of adopting a broader and more nuanced definition of the concept of inspiration emerges, beginning from what the Bible says about itself, not, however, in the sense that in the sacred text there may be parts that are insignificant or without value, but rather in the sense that the charism of inspiration spreads in various ways. It is possible and necessary in any case to accord the tribute of attention and obedience, especially to what more clearly witnesses to Christ and to his perfect message of salvation.

Instead of lessening the adhesion of faith to the Word coming from God, the perspective thus set out promotes its more mature manifestation, because one bows with gratitude for God's self-giving in history and adores the Spirit who has spoken through the prophets (cf. Zech 7:12; Neh 9:30) over the many centuries of salvation history. And, on the other hand, this allows the better understanding of how this Spirit did not cease to operate after the death of the apostles, since it was gifted to the Church so that she might be able to select and appropriate the inspired writings. Such a Spirit is at work today in the act of "hearing the Word of God with reverence" (*DV*, n. 1), because Scripture, according to *Dei Verbum*, n. 12, must "be read and interpreted according to the same Spirit by whom it was written." The inspired Word is to no avail if the one who receives it does not live by the Spirit who appreciates and savors the divine origin of the Bible.

III. The Truth of Sacred Scripture

144. Since it originates in God, Scripture has divine qualities. Among these is the fundamental one of attesting the truth, understood, however, not as an aggregate of exact information on the various aspects of human knowledge but as a revelation of God himself and his salvific plan. The Bible, in fact, makes known the mystery of the Father's love, manifested in the Word made flesh, who, through the Spirit, leads to a perfect communion of human beings with God (*DV*, n. 2).

In this way, it is made clear that the truth of Scripture is that which has the salvation of believers as its goal. The objections—raised in the past and still current today—because of inaccuracies and contradictions of a geographical, historical, and scientific nature, which are rather frequent in the Bible, purport to call into question the reliability of the sacred text and hence its divine origin. These, however, are rejected by the Church in the affirmation that "the books of Scripture must be acknowledged as teaching firmly, faithfully, and without error that truth which God wanted put into the sacred writings for the sake of our salvation" (*DV*, n. 11). It is this truth which gives full meaning to human existence, and it is this which God wanted to be made known to all peoples.

The present document endorses this same hermeneutical perspective; its contribution, innovative only in part, is to show, through an analysis of selected examples carried out on several books of the Bible and on various literary forms, *how* the truth which God intended to reveal to the world through his servants, the sacred authors, is presented.

3.1 Multiform Truth

145. An initial characteristic of biblical truth is that of being expressed in many forms and in various ways (Heb 1:1). Since it is transmitted by many people and in different times, it bears an intrinsically manifold character, both in relation to doctrinal affirmations and norms of behavior and in relation to literary forms. In their historical situation and according to the gift of God, the authors of the sacred text expound what was given them to understand and transmit, and what was spoken by the Lord in the past was combined with new and diverse divine revelations. Moreover, biblical truth embraces a great variety of literary genres, in which we find not only the relevant dogmatic proposition but also the truth proper to the account, that of the legislative norm or the parable, that of the text of a prayer, that of a love poem like the Song of Songs, that of the critique of Job or Qoheleth, or that of the apocalyptic books. Moreover, within these same literary genres, the various points of view, undoubtedly more evident than a simple repetitive convergence, are obvious to all.

This multiform manifestation of divine truth should not be restricted to the literature of the Old Testament but should be recognized also as regards the revelation attested in the New Testament, where we have narrative and discursive forms which hardly overlap and where we observe significant differences in the presentation of the message. We have, in fact, four gospels, and the Church has rejected as erroneous the attempt to find a concordant solution. What is written as the Gospel "according to Luke," for example, should be respected and supported, even if it does not coincide exactly with what Mark or John say. In addition, while for the gospels the message is based essentially on the life of Jesus and his words, for Paul the truth of Christ is rooted almost exclusively in the event of his death and resurrection. And the diversity of presentation between the letter to the Romans and the letter of James is paradigmatic of the plurality through which Scripture attests the unique truth of God.

This polyphony of sacred voices is offered to the Church as a model so that she might acquire, in the present, that same capacity to combine the unity of the message to be transmitted to humanity, with the necessary respect for the multiform varieties of individual experiences, cultures, and gifts bestowed by God.

3.2 Truth in Historical Form

146. A second important character of biblical truth is expressed by its configuration in *historical* form. Several books of Scripture carry indications of the period in which they were written; in other cases, scientific exegesis plausibly places them in various historical periods. The span of time encompassed by the literature of the Bible is without doubt very extensive, since it goes beyond a millennium; it necessarily reveals the legacy of concepts tied to a particular era, of opinions which are the fruit of experiences or concerns characteristic of a particular period of the People of God. The work done by the redactors to give a certain doctrinal and practical coherence to the sacred text did not at all eliminate the traces of history but reveals its uncertainties and imperfections, both in the area of theology and in that of anthropology. The duty of the interpreter is to avoid a fundamentalist reading of Scripture so as to situate the

various formulations of the sacred text in their historical context, according to the literary genres then in vogue. It is by embracing this characteristic of divine revelation that we are actually led to the mystery of Christ, the full and definitive manifestation of the truth of God in human history.

3.3 Canonical Truth

147. The Catholic perspective on interpreting the Bible also maintains that God's truth should be received within the whole context of revelation attested in the *canon* of Sacred Scripture. This means that the revealed truth cannot be limited to a part of the sacred patrimony (rejecting, for example, the Old Testament to affirm the New), nor restricted to a homogeneous nucleus which would eliminate what remains or would relativize it as being of little significance. Not only is all that is inspired necessary for the full revelation of God, but every part must be read in relationship to the other parts, according to a principle of harmony which is to be identified not with uniformity but rather with the pleasing convergence of dissimilarities.

It is clear, however, that from the Christian perspective, the truth of the biblical writing is handed on in the testimony on the *Lord Jesus*, the "Mediator and at the same time the fullness of all revelation" (*DV*, n. 2), he who defines himself as "the way, the truth, and the life" (John 14:6). This essential centrality of the mystery of Christ does not exclude but rather exalts the ancient traditions, which, as Christ himself asserts, speak of him (cf. John 5:39) and of the definitive salvation accomplished in his death and resurrection. In his infinite mystery, Christ is the center which sheds light on the whole of Scripture.

IV. The Literary Traditions of Other Religions

148. Here a glimmer of light reveals itself on how to understand the relationship between Sacred Scripture and the literary traditions of other religions. Such a question is of pressing relevance today for interreligious dialogue; its solution is obviously not easy, because

one must combine the fundamental principle of the "uniqueness and universality of the mystery of Jesus Christ and the Church" (as the title of the declaration *Dominus Iesus* of the Congregation for the Doctrine of the Faith states) with the proper appreciation for the spiritual treasures of other religions. The present document has not spoken explicitly about the ways which, starting from Sacred Scripture itself, could be suggested for the theological and pastoral attention of the Church. However, it may suffice to recall the figure of Balaam (Num 24) to highlight how (inspired) prophecy is not the exclusive prerogative of the people of God and to recall how Saint Paul, in his discourse on the Areopagus, expressed his wholehearted agreement with the intuitions of Greek poets and philosophers (cf. Acts 17:28). On the other hand, it is fully recognized that the literature of the Old Testament is greatly indebted to Mesopotamian and Egyptian writings, just as the New Testament books draw extensively on the cultural heritage of the Hellenistic world. The *semina Verbi* (*Seeds of the Word*) are scattered throughout the world, and cannot therefore be confined to the text of the Bible alone. The Church has defined what she holds to be inspired, but she has not pronounced negatively on all the rest. However, it is the Word of God handed down in the canonical Scriptures, in particular in that part which testifies directly to the Word made flesh, that provides the principle of discernment of the truth of every other religious attestation, both in the Church and in the diverse religious traditions of the various peoples of the earth.

As is clear from these considerations the Church draws life from an efficacious hermeneutical circle; she draws the principles of her beliefs from hearing the words of Scripture, and illuminated by that faith she is made capable not only of correctly interpreting what she reads as her holy book but also of evaluating every other testimony that requires a hearing. It is the role of the Spirit to be that principle of truth which sets in motion the course of belief and brings it to completion, in an indefinite openness to the self-manifestation of God in history.

V. The Interpretation of Difficult Parts of the Bible

149. It is the Church, therefore, the living body of believing readers, the authorized interpreters of the inspired text, which, at

all times and so also today, mediates the reception and proclamation of the truth of Sacred Scripture. Since the Church is endowed with the Holy Spirit, she is truly "the pillar and bulwark of truth" (1 Tim 3:15), to the extent that she faithfully transmits to the world the Word which constitutes her. Her ministry is carried out in the boldness (*parresia*) of the announcement, which proclaims Jesus Christ as the sole and definitive Savior (Acts 4:12). But it is also the duty of the Church in her role as teacher to help the faithful and those in search of truth to interpret correctly the biblical texts by means of suitable methodologies and appropriate hermeneutical assumptions. In this respect, the previous document of the Pontifical Biblical Commission, *The Interpretation of the Bible in the Church*, is particularly useful.

For some time, in fact, some reservations concerning the biblical tradition have become more persistent, because some of its pages and literary trends appear unacceptable to the contemporary conscience because of ideas deemed outdated, customs and juridical practices regarded as controversial or downright reprehensible, and narrations that seem to lack historical foundation. This has led to a widespread discrediting of the sacred text and a veiled mistrust of its pastoral usefulness, to the point of actually calling into question the inspiration of certain parts of the Bible (and, by extension, their truth). Hence, it is not enough to assert in a general way that "incomplete and temporary" things are found in the Old Testament (*DV*, n. 15), or to recall that the writers of the New Testament too were influenced by the mentality of their age; if we can restate the principle of incarnation, applying it analogously to the commitment to writing of divine revelation, it is also necessary to indicate how, in this very human weakness, the glory of the divine Word nonetheless shines forth. It is not sufficient either to eliminate the problematic passages from public reading in the liturgical assembly for the sake of a prudent pastoral concern; those who know the text as a whole may even resent the curtailment of the sacred patrimony or may accuse pastors of concealing unjustifiably the difficult aspects of the Bible.

150. The Church cannot draw back from the humble and arduous task of interpreting in a respectful way the entire literary tradition which she defines as inspired and, therefore, an expression of

God's truth. Interpretation requires above all the establishment of clear principles which help to understand that the meaning of what has been handed down does not immediately coincide with the "letter" of the text. On the other hand, it is necessary to proceed in an orderly way, dealing one by one with the problems that need to be solved, so that one can express the necessary commitment of the believer to make the Word of God one's own, according to the gift of intelligence which the Holy Spirit imparts in every period of history.

For this reason this document of the Pontifical Biblical Commission has chosen a few of the major problems that cause difficulties for today's reader and has suggested some possible ways for their interpretation within the framework of our faith. The brevity of the treatment may not always be satisfactory, but the hermeneutical principles set forth here should prove helpful, as should some points on specific questions.

Rather than a definitive and exhaustive examination of the difficult problems found in the Scriptures, what is formulated here is a possible hermeneutical strategy with the intention of provoking further reflection in dialogue with other interpreters of the sacred text. In our common research effort, the path toward the truth will turn out to be more humble and, at the same time, more luminous, since it will be pervaded by a reciprocal attention to the same Spirit.

Scriptural Index